The Portfolio

Seriously useful guides

The Portfolio
An Architecture Student's Handbook

*Igor Marjanović, Katerina Rüedi Ray
and Lesley Naa Norle Lokko*

ELSEVIER

Architectural
Press

AMSTERDAM • BOSTON • HEIDELBERG • LONDON • NEW YORK • OXFORD
PARIS • SAN DIEGO • SAN FRANCISCO • SINGAPORE • SYDNEY • TOKYO
Architectural Press is an imprint of Elsevier

Architectural Press
An imprint of Elsevier
Linacre House, Jordan Hill, Oxford OX2 8DP
30 Corporate Drive, Burlington, MA 01803

First published 2003
Reprinted 2004, 2005

British Library Cataloguing in Publication Data
A catalogue record for this book is available from the British Library

Library of Congress Cataloguing in Publication Data
A catalogue record for this book is available from the Library of Congress

ISBN 0 7506 5764 2

For information on all Architectural Press publications visit
our website at www.architecturalpress.com

Working together to grow
libraries in developing countries

www.elsevier.com | www.bookaid.org | www.sabre.org

ELSEVIER   BOOK AID International   Sabre Foundation

Printed and bound in Great Britain by MPG Books Ltd, Bodmin, Cornwall

Contents

About the Authors

Igor Marjanović is Adjunct Assistant Professor of Architecture and Interim Director of Undergraduate Studies at the University of Illinois at Chicago. He has practiced and exhibited widely, including Europe, South and North America. Igor's design awards include those from the Chicago Architectural Club, the Art Institute of Chicago, Universities UK, and the International Union of Architects (UIA). His research focuses on travel, hybridity, and the appropriation of montage practices in architectural design. He is working on a book which explores the relationship between architectural and cinematic montage. With Katerina Rüedi Ray he is one of ten selected exhibitors in the forthcoming architectural exhibition *Chicago: Issues for a New Millennium at the Art Institute of Chicago*. Igor studied architecture at the University of Belgrade, Serbia, the Moscow Architectural Institute, Russia, and the University of Illinois at Chicago, USA. He is currently undertaking research for his PhD by Design at the Bartlett School of Architecture, University College London, UK.

Katerina Rüedi Ray is the Director of the School of Art at Bowling Green State University. From 1996 to 2002 she was the Director of the School of Architecture at the University of Illinois at Chicago. She studied architecture at the Architectural Association in London, UK and has a masters and a doctoral degree in architecture from University College London, UK. She has taught architectural design and theory at the Architectural Association, the Bartlett School and Kingston University, UK. She has won various European design awards and she has acted as a visiting professor, critic and lecturer at numerous European and north-American architecture and art schools. Her publications include *Desiring Practices: Architecture, Gender and the Interdisciplinary, Desiring Practices: Artists and Architects* and *The Dissertation: An Architecture Student's Handbook.* She is currently working on several books, including *Chicago is History, Bauhaus Dream-house: Identity Formation in Modernist Design Education,* and *133 and Rising: African-American Women Architects.* With Igor Marjanović she is one of ten selected exhibitors in the forthcoming architectural exhibition *Chicago: Issues for a New Millennium at the Art Institute of Chicago.*

Lesley Naa Norle Lokko is Course Director of the MArch. programme in Cultural Identity, Globalization and Architecture at the Bartlett School of Architecture, University College London, UK. Lesley studied architecture at the Bartlett, UCL where she also taught for two years before moving to the USA to teach at Iowa State University and at the University of Illinois at Chicago. On her return to the UK in 2000, she taught at Kingston University and was the Academic Leader at University of North London before re-joining the Bartlett in 2002. She is the author of *White Papers, Black Marks: Race, Culture, Architecture* and has published and lectured widely on the subject of race, cultural identity and diasporic cultures and how these inform architectural and spatial production. She is a founder member of ThirdSpace, an organization which aims to provide a forum for architects and academics interested in issues of architecture and postcolonial/cultural studies. She has also just written her first novel (*Sundowners*, due for publication January 2004) and now divides her time between academia and fiction writing.

Acknowledgements

We wish to offer our sincere thanks to Dr Jonathan Hill for his assistance at various times in this project. We also wish to thank the various tutors and professors who have worked with the authors whose portfolios appear in the book, as well as, most importantly the authors themselves. In addition, we wish to thank Anthony Marty for his design and technical assistance relating to the web page accompanying the book, and James McKay for technical assistance with the many digital glitches we encountered. We are also sincerely grateful to Alison Yates and Elizabeth Whiting, of Elsevier, for their consistently helpful advice. Finally, and most importantly, we wish to thank Jasna Marjanović and Roger Ray for their unfailing support in a myriad ways throughout all stages of this project.

Igor Marjanović
Katerina Rüedi Ray
Lesley Naa Norle Lokko

List of illustrations

Chapter 6

Chapter 7

1 Introduction

Why Make a Portfolio?

A carefully wrought portfolio of work will be the single most important record and outcome of your architectural education. The major part of your education is always going to be the design of buildings as executed through drawings, models and other kinds of visual representation, and your portfolio records the ideas, the processes and the result of your work as a designer in the architecture studio as well as in other visually oriented classes. It can also contain other kinds of information, from your professional work in an architectural office, to your creative work in related artistic disciplines, your built work if you have construction experience, and your written work if that is an important part of your educational process. It is a document with many functions and will therefore take different shapes depending on the situation for which you need it. If it is well considered and crafted it will certainly open many doors for you – to further study, to different areas of work in the architectural profession, and quite possibly work in related fields. You will also need it to get teaching positions in academia, or in secondary (UK) or high school (USA) education. It can also help you win prizes and scholarships while you are on your way.

Whichever purpose it needs to serve, your portfolio is your passport and your visiting card, through which you introduce yourself to the new worlds you wish to enter and by which your value is established and compared to others. Very importantly, it is also a document through which you make a contribution to how we

> **understand architecture; it is your chance to clarify and share what you believe and aspire to, and to present new ideas, techniques, observations and experiences, mainly to others but sometimes just to yourself.**

The Handbook

This handbook provides a guide to the whole process of designing, making and sending out or presenting a portfolio. It explains carefully what to do, how to do it, when to do it, and what the major pitfalls are to avoid when making a portfolio. Each university and architectural programme does, of course, have its own rules and requirements for a portfolio. Architectural offices also vary in what they like to see in a portfolio. Sometimes these requirements are explicit, and sometimes they are less tangible. Whichever the case, you are strongly advised to check everything said here with what different institutions and offices expect. It is also important for you to understand that sometimes the advice we will offer you may differ from that given by your professors or colleagues in an architectural office. This is because the architectural discipline is becoming more and more pluralistic in its ideas and cultures, and architectural portfolios necessarily reflect that pluralism. Even if it were once possible, there is no longer a single type or format of portfolio that will fit all contexts. Instead you will need to make choices depending on the destination or design culture for which the portfolio is intended. Nonetheless, if you follow the guidance in this book, and if you add to it your own intelligent and rigorous creative efforts, you should go on to produce a portfolio of the best possible standard for the different situations in which portfolios are needed.

The book, following this introduction, is divided into five chapters.

Chapter 2 Getting Started outlines the essential ideas behind a portfolio, the kind of occasions for which you need to prepare different portfolios, different kinds of specialization in architecture, and how you might adjust the message of your portfolio to the audience that will be looking at it.

Chapter 3 Design Cultures explains why portfolios differ in form and content in different design cultures, and how they represent cultural value. It gives some practical advice about how to find out about the design cultures of different architectural schools and practices, and how to understand some regional and global differences.

Chapter 4 Academic Portfolio then focuses in detail on how to prepare an academic portfolio, what it needs to contain, and how to format an academic CV, statement of intent, references and letters of recommendation.

Chapter 5 Professional Portfolio examines in detail how to prepare a professional portfolio, covering portfolio form and content, résumé, references and the cover letter, with special emphasis on the selection and presentation of built work.

Chapter 6 Preparing Material offers practical advice on selecting, recording and storing work, as well as scanning, reducing and reproducing it.

Chapter 7 The Folio Container is about making the physical portfolio container itself, whether this is bought or made specially for the occasion.

Chapter 8 Making the Traditional Portfolio gives advice about the organization and layout of images and text in the portfolio for a small selection of different portfolio types.

Chapter 9 Digital Portfolio focuses on the advantages and disadvantages of the digital portfolio, as well as different formats such as CDs or web pages, and outlines some basic technical issues related to the digital production of images and animations.

The final chapter, Chapter 10 Afterwards gives advice about how best to send your portfolio, whether in physical or digital format, and also suggests useful ways to keep updating your portfolio.

Throughout this book, we are very proud to say, you will also find examples of pages from outstanding portfolios previously completed by architecture students. Some of these are prizewinning portfolios submitted to the Royal Institute of British Architects in London for its international Presidents Silver and Bronze Medal student competition. Others are award winners in the Skidmore Owings and Merrill Travelling Fellowship, the most important architectural competition for USA students. Other portfolios helped their authors to obtain work in architectural practice, in architectural education, or in related design disciplines such as graphic design or advertising. You will therefore find not only pertinent advice but also instances of how architectural students have tackled the portfolio with extremely successful results. We have tried to point out individual strategies used by the contributors in their portfolios in captions below the images at the end of each chapter. These groups of images will give you a quick visual introduction to some of the issues covered in each chapter. However, you will still need to read each chapter itself to get a balanced overview of the issues it covers.

Accompanying this book is a website that shows the full portfolios of the contributors to this book. In many instances it also includes the contributors' résumés or curriculum vitae so that you can get an idea how to format those for yourself. We encourage you to go to the website to get the overall impression of each portfolio, as individual pages certainly do not do justice to the creativity, thoughtfulness, technical ability and hard work that have gone into the making of each of these portfolios. The website url is http://www.theportfolio.org.uk

The website will also give you an idea of the diversity of formats and approaches which you can explore as you prepare your portfolio. We hope that it will help and encourage you to make your portfolio a document of which you will be proud and which will represent you well in the broader world of architecture and design.

2 Getting Started

Getting started involves understanding the most basic aspects of a portfolio and its preparation. Getting started also involves understanding why you need a portfolio and what it is for. This chapter will help you get started, outlining some of the issues to help tailor your portfolio to various destinations in academia and practice.

What is a Portfolio?

A portfolio of work is defined in different ways depending on the situation. There are different portfolios for different occasions. Obviously you will have one kind of portfolio at the end of your second year as an undergraduate student and another kind when you have finished post-professional studies. More importantly, when you come to make your portfolio at the moments in your life when you want your academic or professional career to develop or change, you will most probably make a different portfolio to suit where you would like to be heading.

However, all these different kinds of portfolios will have one thing in common. They will contain your work in a format that will make it easy for the portfolio to be transported physically and digitally to many different situations. The most normal format for a portfolio most closely resembles a book. It can be a small book (A4 or 8½" × 11" (210 × 279 mm)) which is easy to mail, or it can be a large book, almost like a collection of paintings (A1 or 24" × 36" (594 × 841 mm)) which you take with you to interviews. Increasingly, portfolios are digital and can be sent in CD format or exist as a website. With a digital portfolio you will have more freedom to play with the format but will also be relying on someone else to understand how to access it.

> **Remember, it is still easier for most people to turn pages than to navigate links and understand graphic and animation software.**

All these formats will have one thing in common. The fact that the portfolio is a travelling document, that its function and meaning may change depending on the context, and that your career may hang on it, means that it has to be tough, beautiful, clearly organized, very easy to understand and even easier to use.

Whatever the context for which you need the portfolio, or the phase of your career, there are basic rules about the portfolio that you should remember. They are:

- DOCUMENTATION
- EDITING
- MESSAGE
- AUDIENCE

Documentation

The first rule for making a portfolio is to *keep* every piece of work you produce in the studio, in the office and in related visual, technical, or practical areas. Taking care of your work is the most important professional activity you will ever do. Although you may not see the connection now, later on you may need to show some of your exploratory sketches for a design project because a particular Diploma Course or graduate programme may want to see how you think through drawing. Or you may need construction photographs because a particular office may want to see that you already have some site experience, and that you know how to recognize good from bad construction. So, get into the habit of scanning or photographing hand-drawn work or models at regular points during the project. A good time to do this is immediately after a review or jury – it gives you time to reflect on the totality of the work, and if you do it well, it will make you proud of what you have done. Make sure you date the work – memory alone can play tricks later on. Buy a plan chest (UK) or a flat file (USA) for your flat work. Take photos when you go on site and date them. Keep an album or digital record of photos. Get extra copies of construction drawings that you produced or co-produced. Save all your digital files and make sure you get CD copies of digital work so that your work is always backed up outside as well as inside your computer. Dating, scanning and filing work is good to do when you need a break from creative work. This will create a large volume of work, so think about its ease of storage and transportation. As you are designing, whether you are making sketches, drawings or models, use consistent sizes or plan to assemble work into consistent formats at regular intervals – it will be much easier to transport and store. Having a thousand pieces of work of different sizes will make your life really difficult in the long run.

However you choose to do it, remember: when in doubt, be consistent and DOCUMENT!

Editing

The second rule for making a portfolio, however, is knowing what it is not. The portfolio is definitely not an archive of every piece of work that you have ever done. At a basic practical level you will not have the time and money to reproduce all that work, you will not want to pay vast amounts of money to mail it, and certainly the people who will be looking at your portfolio will not have time to look at everything you have done. In a professional situation, especially if there is an economic recession and greater competition for work, very often if you do not capture in the first few pages of your portfolio the imaginations of the people who are looking at it, they may not even get all the way through your portfolio. That means you will need to edit the portfolio itself to include only the best, the most engaging and sometimes the most provocative, work. In addition, you will need to remember that there are also differences between portfolio expectations in different countries. In the USA the portfolio you will most likely use to apply for entry into graduate school will probably be mailed in and be smaller in size and volume whereas in the UK, where you often take original work or large print-outs to a personal interview, the portfolio can be larger in size and contain more work. In the UK you may be able to explain work in person whereas in the USA you will need to make sure your portfolio will say everything you want your audience to know. Finally, you will need to edit your work because your portfolio will have to be as clear as possible about your ideas and experience, and should only contain work that shows your strengths.

The second rule for making a portfolio is therefore EDIT, EDIT, EDIT!

Message

The third rule for making a portfolio is to know exactly what you want to show and why. As an architectural student you will need a portfolio for different occasions. What you decide to edit out and what you decide to keep in the portfolio will depend on how you want to be seen and what the portfolio is for. What kind of a message are you trying to get across? By this we do not mean a verbal message, although you will almost certainly want to use words to emphasize your focus in your work. A portfolio message should clearly communicate what kind of architectural interests and skills you have. For example, the portfolio you will use to apply to graduate school may emphasize your creativity and ability to work through challenging ideas and unusual forms, whereas a portfolio you use to apply for a professional job in an office may need to include construction drawings, site photographs and schedules to emphasize your technical competence. Even more specifically, if you are applying to a graduate school because you want to join that school's specialization in community architecture or activist practice, you will need to select documents from your vast archive or work which show both a breadth of creativity and your special interest in community architecture. You might include photos of work you have done in community gardens, essays you have written on collaborative practices or public art, and highlight those projects you did as an undergraduate which show that you have an ability to respond to the needs of others. If you are applying to a school where you wish to pursue design and robotics, say, make sure that you include in your portfolio any moving objects you have made, or research essays and reports on the subject. Occasionally this may mean that you might have to make a new project just for the portfolio. If your education to date has not provided you with the kind of work you think you will need to go to the next phase of your career, you may need to take extra evening classes or make additional drawings to show just how committed you are to the direction you want to pursue. For example, if you have a very technical undergraduate portfolio and you want to get into a diploma or graduate school that is very artistic, you may need to take an evening class in sculpture or drawing. Making a portfolio means you are making an identity for yourself, through the work that you select to show.

> The third rule for making a portfolio therefore is to be very clear about THE MESSAGE.

Audience

As you can see, the message of your portfolio will change depending on the next intended phase of your career. The most important thing to remember is that although you, the author of the work, and your message, may remain the same during a particular phase of your career, the audience for your work may change dramatically. In many cases you yourself may want to use the portfolio to change your environment – sometimes dramatically if you are thinking of changing countries or continents to get into graduate school, a postgraduate programme or an architectural office. Your portfolio will need to show not only the message – what you already do well – but how what you do well might fit into the world of the people who will be looking at your work. You need to understand your audience and its conventions before you prepare the portfolio. If you do that you will have the best chance possible to communicate appropriately. This chapter, as well as Chapters 3 and 4 focus on this in more detail, as the audiences for your portfolio will definitely have a significant impact on the format and content of the portfolio.

> The fourth and most important rule for making the portfolio is therefore to understand THE AUDIENCE.

To help you understand this a little better, here are some of the most common types of occasions for which you will need to prepare a portfolio.

Entering and Passing the Academic Year/Portfolio Review

Although some schools of architecture require portfolios for admission into a degree course in the UK, or the undergraduate programme in the USA, it is more likely that preparing for a portfolio review will probably be the first time you will need to make a portfolio. Nevertheless, if you are applying to an undergraduate programme or degree course that requires a portfolio, most of the advice in this book will apply to you as well. The main difference will be that your portfolio will most likely have work from your art or drafting class, or visual and constructed work you have made in your free time. Schools that ask for a portfolio for admission to the first or freshman year are usually pretty clear about the format, so make sure you ask exactly what they are looking for. The rules for passing the academic year vary from school to school and can appear more, or less, mysterious depending on the school. In most UK schools of architecture, passing the academic year is based on some form of portfolio review, but the format is not always specified, and you may or may not be present at the review. In USA schools you may pass your individual courses, including the design studio, based on grades given by each of your professors, but may also need to go through a portfolio review to get feedback on your overall progress or even to be admitted to higher level classes. In the USA this kind of review is usually based on a selection of your work that has been reduced and formatted into a booklet, most often 8½" × 11" (210 × 297 mm) and it is unusual for you to be present at the review. In the UK you will be more likely to submit your actual work, in a large A1 or A2 portfolio case, or even present it as a degree or diploma exhibition, to your professors and external examiners. Again, check with your school, and ask other students for advice.

Whichever format you may need, in both cases you should edit out material that does not show your strengths. Focus on communicating your successes, but also make sure that you have a breadth of work, as most architecture schools are looking for signs of continuing improvement in integrating different information within design projects. Choose work that shows your ideas and skills, and your ability to combine complex issues into a coherent whole, thus making your design as easy to understand as possible. Use text clearly and minimally for maximum impact. The most important thing to remember about the portfolio review process is that the focus is on showing your design skills and the development of your work over the relevant period of time. The people who will be looking at your portfolio will be professors or design tutors, who are interested in your development as a student. If you can, make friends with students in senior years, and look at their portfolios. If your school keeps work for validation or accreditation, or has a Year-End-Show, or keeps portfolio examples, make sure you see this and understand why the good work is good. Do not be afraid to ask your professors and older students for advice. You will find a lot more information about this in Chapter 4 Academic Portfolio.

Getting/Changing a Job in an Architect's Office

If you are an undergraduate student, the next kind of portfolio you will need to prepare will be the one that presents your work to potential employers. Here, your audience will be looking for your capacity to be useful in their architectural office so your message needs to emphasize your competence and compatibility with their work. If you have any kind of construction experience, such as helping your family build a house extension, or have worked for architects or contractors while at school, it is essential that you include copies of drawings or models or building elements that you made. For example, once you have had some office experience, you may wish to include a selection, or even a full set, of construction drawings. Offices are also interested in your design work at school, particularly if you have done design or other work in areas which the office has as a specialization. For example, if you have done housing design at school, and the office to which you are applying has a strong record in housing, make sure you highlight housing work in your folio. If you have done projects on mass-customization and are applying to offices that specialize in this, show it. Whereas in academia you might just capture someone's attention if you come across as a bit of an eccentric, offices will be very interested in your capacity to communicate clearly and succinctly. That means making your portfolio very simple to understand. Chapter 5 Professional Portfolio is devoted to the professional market and has more information about this.

Getting into a Diploma Course (Graduate School)

Probably the most important time you will prepare a portfolio as a student will be when you will try to change schools. Most graduate programmes or diploma courses have more applicants than places, and in the best schools the competition is intense. Here your work will need to have something in common with the strengths of the school, and it will also need to stand out from the crowd. Make sure your major interests are clearly represented, and if you think you are short on work that shows what you can do, do additional work for the portfolio. Chris Ciraulo's portfolio of academic work from the University of Illinois at Chicago (Figures 2.1 and 2.2) was made for admission to a Graduate Programme in the USA. It emphasizes strong computer graphic skills while demonstrating a variety of representational media: drawings, models, text, etc. It enabled him to get a scholarship to attend a graduate programme with an outstanding tradition in digital media. Chapter 4 is devoted to the portfolio in the Academy and has more information about this.

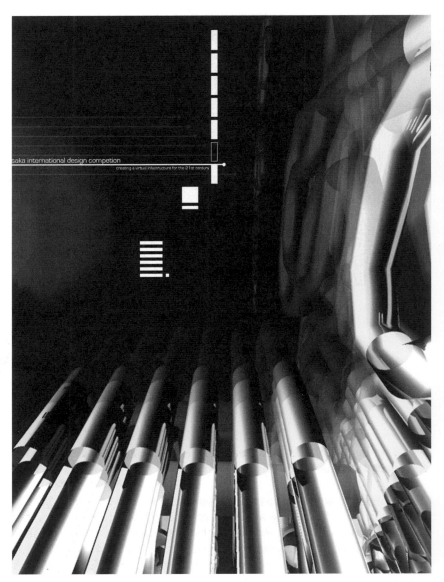

Figure 2.1
Christopher Ciraulo, Osaka International Design Competition

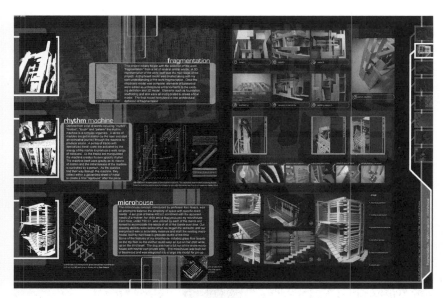

Figure 2.2
Christopher Ciraulo, collage of undergraduate work from the University of
Illinois at Chicago, IL, USA, showing the development of design ideas
through drawings, models, and text

Winning Scholarships and Teaching/Research/Graduate Assistantships

Competition for scholarships and assistantships is even more intense.
These are more frequently available at graduate level in the USA, but
generally rare in the UK. Whatever the case, your portfolio will have
to be outstanding to get you into the pool for such funding. There will
need to be a close fit between your work and the school, and your
work will need to be of a very high standard indeed. Each page will
need to capture attention immediately, highlight your ideas, and show
their originality and relevance to the agenda of the school. For
example, a strong undergraduate digital portfolio will help you to get
graduate support at a school where digital media form a central part
of teaching and research, such as the Massachusetts Institute of
Technology (MIT).

Winning Fellowships and Prizes

Competition for national student prizes and teaching fellowships is tougher still. Being selected by your school for competitions like the RIBA Bronze or Silver Medal, or the Skidmore Owings and Merrill prize, is already an enormous acknowledgement of your talent. Winning means that you have successfully competed nationally and internationally with many other outstanding students of your generation. It can open doors to great jobs in practice and the academy. You need to remember that different prizes and fellowships have different portfolio requirements but are usually very specific about quantity and format of the work, so in general do not try to bend the rules. Instead, your editing and your message have to be carefully thought through so that the attention of your audience (the jury) is captured immediately. Once you have made it through the first round (where work is usually eliminated fairly quickly) your projects will need to stand closer scrutiny. The project pages will need to be well-composed, the project will need to be well-described and the design will need to be consistently outstanding. Projects that win such prizes usually have a strong idea, and consistent and detailed follow through. If you need to see examples of the very best work, the RIBA Silver and Bronze Medals web page has images of work by recent winners. Jeff Morgan's portfolio of work from the University of Illinois at Chicago won the Schiff Award, a highly competitive award for Midwestern schools of architecture in the USA and it shows how a clear graphic layout can be successfully used to achieve a high level of consistency between the boards (see Figures 2.3 and 2.4). His portfolio also demonstrates an ability to easily bridge between concept and detail, and his ability to bring each project to the high level of completion.

Architectural Fellowships/Prizes References
The RIBA Silver and Bronze Medial, RIBA, London, UK. Website: http://www.presidentsmedals.com/
Skidmore, Owings, and Merrill Award, The SOM Foundation, Chicago/ London. Website: www.som.com

Getting/Changing a Job in Related Fields

An architectural education prepares you for professional life not only in architecture; it can also help you enter related fields such as graphic design, advertising, film, construction, real estate, and so on. If you

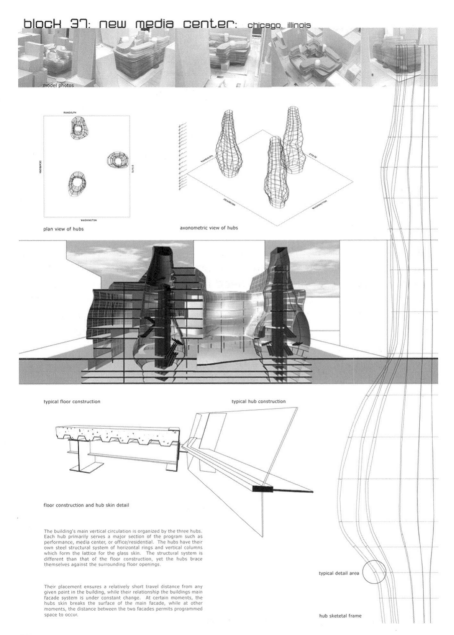

Figure 2.3
Jeffrey Morgan, Block 37: New Media Center, Chicago, IL, USA work from
the M.Arch program at the University of Illinois at Chicago, IL, USA. Schiff
Award 2001

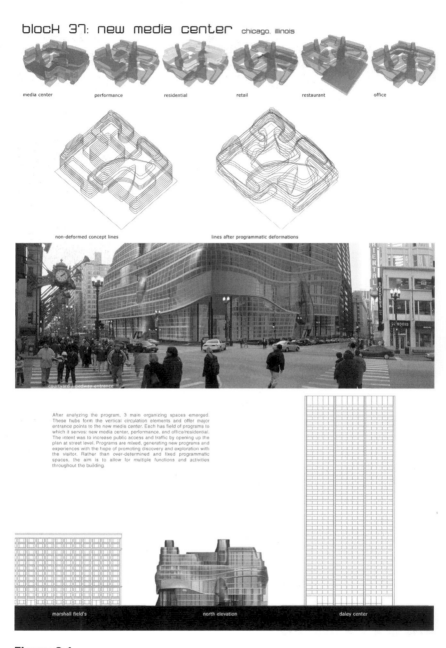

Figure 2.4
Jeffrey Morgan, Block 37: New Media Center, Chicago, IL, USA, Schiff Award, 2001

Figure 2.5
Anthony Max D. Marty, portfolio of Undergraduate work in the B.Arch
program of the Illinois Institute of Technology, Chicago, Il, USA

are thinking of making such a change, your portfolio will need to show
some evidence of skills and ideas related to your chosen field. For
example, if you are trying to get a position in a related discipline like
graphic design, your folio may include, beside architectural projects,
graphic compositions, and experiments with book formats and layouts,
and even different portfolio types. Anthony Marty's portfolio of design
work from the Illinois Institute of Technology (Figure 2.5) demonstrates an early interest in graphic design, composition, container
design and visual imagery, which is helpful if you are thinking of
seeking employment in the graphic design field. Chapter 3 discusses
this in more detail. Whichever area you choose to enter, it helps to
show that you have studied it, or have some experience of working
in it, demonstrated through the work shown in your portfolio.

Getting a Teaching Job

Finally, you will need a portfolio when you are applying for teaching
positions. Here you will need to show not only your own design work,

but also your written work, including published essays or projects. Preparing a portfolio for getting a teaching job is a big job, as there are significant differences between expectations in different countries and at different levels of teaching. In the USA, in particular, there are very specific things that a school will be looking to find in your portfolio depending on what type of position you are seeking, which will have a major impact on its organization, and on the way that you organize your CV. Teaching positions are hard to get, and therefore you will be facing stiff competition. Make sure that your portfolio reflects the requirements of the position that is advertised, but sending a portfolio to the head or director of the school can sometimes help you obtain a part-time or adjunct teaching position without a position being advertised. If you have been a teaching assistant, you might want to include copies of your syllabi and work produced by your best students. Chapter 3 has a lot more information about this.

Other kinds of portfolios

There is one kind of portfolio that this book does not address because that would be the subject of a whole book in its own right. The practice portfolio, whether in printed or digital form, on CD or as a web page, is an essential document that, as you become an independent architectural practitioner, will one day represent your professional work. Learning how to make an academic or professional portfolio of the highest standard will provide a good basis for you to create a practice portfolio later on. And each time you reformat your student portfolio you will also refine your message and learn to understand the conventions of the different areas of the architectural discipline – becoming clearer about the destinations and audiences you wish to reach.

Portfolio Destinations

As we have already said, the portfolio is the single most important document in your architectural education and practice. It is a medium that will help you get to various professional destinations. Architectural practices are becoming increasingly diverse, and it is very important that you become familiar with what the choices are. It is precisely because of that diversity that it is very hard to categorize contemporary architectural practices, but for the purposes of this handbook we will outline some of the main movements in architectural education and design practice. Once you are familiar with these movements, try to research them in more depth – look for precedents, examples, and offices that practice them. Try to understand their aesthetic, imagery, and vocabulary, because if you are planning to join them it is very important to understand how they work and communicate. Look for the types of images such offices use, types of software they prefer, ideas they are referring to, etc.

The situation is very similar with graduate schools. Some of them even have concentrations or specializations that closely follow some of these movements. When you look at the prospective schools for your postgraduate education, check if they have concentrations and if they do, try to tailor your portfolio towards one of their concentrations. This will demonstrate your understanding of contemporary practices, and it will also demonstrate your desire to expand your design research. Following are the outlines of some of the main movements and aesthetics in architectural design, with a list of some basic readings, monographs, and architectural practices. Please note that some of the website addresses might have changed since the first publication of this book.

This list is by no means complete, so if an area of specialization offered by a school or a practice is not included in this book, use a similar methodology to the one we use below to find the references and practices of your specialization interest. Then make sure you are as educated as possible about the specialization before you start preparing the portfolio.

Architectural Technologies

Architectural technologies explore the relationships between architecture, materials and technology, illustrating the impact of new technologies and materials on architectural design, construction, management and use. This is a major area of specialization in architecture, and many schools of architecture include courses and studios in this area, such as building science, structures, materials science, environmental systems, acoustics and lighting. Some schools that are recognized as being strong in this area are Sheffield Hallam University (UK), South Bank University (UK), the Illinois Institute of Technology (USA), and the Massachusetts Institute of Technology (USA). Katrin Klingenberg's portfolio, for example, demonstrates interest in materials and construction through successful use of examples of her own built work (see Figure 2.6).

Figure 2.6
Nicholas Smith and Katrin Klingenberg, collage of construction joints and
materials

Architectural Technologies References

Harris, J. *et al.* Intelligent Skins, Oxford: Architectural Press, 2001
Sebestyen, G. *et al.* New Architecture and Technology, Oxford:
    Architectural Press, 2003

Architectural Technologies Practices

Arup Associates, London, UK. Website: www.arupassociates.com/
Wilkinson Eyre, London, UK. Website: www.wilkinsoneyre.com/
Murphy Jahn Architects, Chicago, IL, USA. Website:
    http://www.murphyjahn.com/intro.htm

Digital Media

With the advance of information technology, architects are becoming increasingly interested in digital media. Digital media make extensive use of digital technologies to address questions regarding the relationship between actual and virtual environments, and actively pursue alternative forms of architectural and urban space. Digital media deal with electronically based methods and techniques of design and construction, thus questioning traditional formal, material, and programatic aspects of architecture. Generally speaking, digital media have two aspects: virtual reality and digital fabrication. Virtual reality utilizes various animation softwares, such as Maya, Softimage, 3D Studio Max/Viz, and Form Z, in order to speculate about new kinds of space. On the other hand, some of these programs can also be used to build models through laser cutters and ultimately to fabricate structures. Some of the schools that have concentrations in these areas are: Architectural Association (London, UK), The Bartlett School of Architecture (London, UK), Columbia University (New York City, USA), Sci-Arc (Los Angeles, USA), University of Illinois at Chicago (USA), Massachusetts Institute of Technology – MIT (Cambridge, USA), University of California at Los Angeles (UCLA, USA), etc. If you are interested in digital media, it is obvious that you will need to show in your portfolio evidence of interest in and understanding of, CAD software, theories of virtual environments, and so on. Even more importantly, your portfolio may primarily have a digital format, while demonstrating interest to pursue research agendas in digital design and fabrication. RED's portfolio demonstrates an interest in digital media through use of 3D models and digital diagrams, and is a continuation of their academic work done at the Architectural Association, London (see Figure 2.7).

Figure 2.7
RED (A. Ramirez and D. Stojanović), Development of design ideas through various forms of 3D modeling and animations

Digital Media References
Beckmann, John. The Virtual Dimension – Architecture, Representation and Crash Culture. New York: Princeton Architectural Press, 1998
Brayer, Marie-Ange; Simonot, Beatrice (Editors). Archilab's Futurehouse: Radical Experiments in Living Space. London: Thames and Hudson, 2002
Engeli, Maia (Editor). Bits and Spaces: CAAD for Physical, Virtual and Hybrid Architecture at ETH Zurich. Basel: Birkhauser Architectural Press, 2001
Lynn, Greg. Animate Form. New York: Princeton Architectural Press, 1999
Migayrou, Frederic; Brayer, Marie-Ange (Editors). Archilab: Radical Experiments in Global Architecture. London: Thames and Hudson, 2001
Neale, John; Porter, Tom. Architectural Supermodels: Physical Design Simulation. Oxford: Architectural Press, 2000.
Zellner, Peter. Hybrid Space – New Forms in Digital Architecture. New York: Rizzoli, 1999.

Digital Medial Practices
Studio Asymptote, Lise Ann-Couture and Hani Rashid, Principals, New York City, USA. Web address: http://www.asymptote-architecture.com/
Greg Lynn FORM, Greg Lynn, Principal, Venice, California, USA. Web address: http://www.glform.com/
Garofalo Architects, Douglas Garofalo, Principal, Chicago, USA. Web address: http://garofalo.a-node.net/home.htm
Oosterhuis.nl, Kas Oosterhuis, Principal, Rotterdam, The Netherlands. Web address: http://www.oosterhuis.nl/
UN Studio, (Van Berkel & Bos Architectuurbureau), Ben van Berkel and Caroline Bos, Directors, Amsterdam, The Netherlands. Web address: http://www.unstudio.com/
cj lim Studio 8, cj lim, Principal, London, United Kingdom. Web address: http://www.cjlim-studio8.com

Landscape Urbanism, Contemporary Urbanism and Urban Design

As architects, you will not only deal with structures, but will also work at much larger scales which cover the city and sometimes even whole regions. Landscape urbanism works across scales and deals with the integration of urban landscape and infrastructure, while looking for ways of articulating the public space. Landscape urbanism is interdisciplinary in its character, bringing together architects, planners, landscape architects, ecologists, engineers, etc. Landscape Urbanism focuses on the design of buildings, open spaces and landscapes, as well as elements of urban infrastructure. Landscape urbanism design studios often pair up with courses in urban theory, urban ecology, and history of the urban landscape. It is important to say that these are not traditional landscape architecture programmes. Rather, landscape urbanism looks at the contemporary city and its problems and tries to define the possible contributions that architects, as part of interdisciplinary teams, can make to its long-term sustainability. Some of the schools that have this specialization are the Architectural Association (London, UK), University of Illinois at Chicago (USA), etc. If you wish to enter this area, you will need to show interest in and understanding of the integration of site strategies, architectural ideas, landscape principles and ecological knowledge.

One related area is contemporary urbanism. In this area architects look at the city and its current problems and try to respond to aspects of popular culture and everyday streetscape. As well as designing beautiful structures, such architects also utilize shock-effect techniques to propose big structures derived from everyday consumer culture. Since they work with large-scale buildings and open urban spaces, their work sometimes intersects with the agendas of landscape urbanism. Here your folio will need to show how you understand and use large-scale urban phenomena, especially those related to consumer culture, tourism, travel, and so on. Some schools that have this specialization are Harvard Graduate School of Design (USA), Berlage Institute (Rotterdam, The Netherlands), and Delft Institute of Technology (The Netherlands).

Yet another area is urban design. This area is well-established, but differs enormously between the USA and UK. In the USA urban design mainly centres on the production of urban policy on transportation, employment, taxation, and so forth, with little or no visual exploration of the consequences of urban policy decisions. In the UK, urban design has a strong visual component, and schools of architecture may have urban design specializations, and for entry to these you may need a portfolio. Urban design can intersect with contemporary urbanism as well as landscape urbanism depending on the school. Some schools that have this specialization are Oxford Brookes University (UK), London School of Economics (UK), and Washington University (St. Louis, USA), As with landscape urbanism and contemporary urbanism,

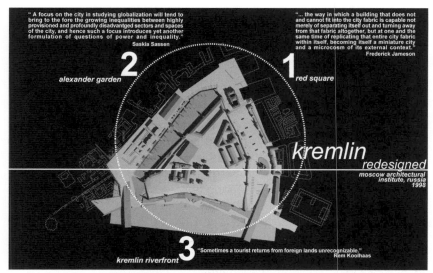

" A focus on the city in studying globalization will tend to bring to the fore the growing inequalities between highly provisioned and profoundly disadvantged sectors and spaces of the city, and hence such a focus introduces yet another formulation of questions of power and inequality."
Saskia Sassen

"... the way in which a building that does not and cannot fit into the city fabric is capable not merely of separating itself out and turning away from that fabric altogether, but at one and the same time of replicating that entire city fabric within itself, becoming itself a miniature city and a microcosm of its external context."
Frederick Jameson

2 alexander garden

1 red square

kremlin redesigned
moscow architectural institute, russia 1998

3 kremlin riverfront

"Sometimes a tourist returns from foreign lands unrecognizable."
Rem Koolhaas

The project establishes an architectural design process for the informational age. This particular way of computer-based designing was the result of a globalized architectural practice. The main task was to design a democratic and accessible space. The site, which is located around the Kremlin walls, is composed of three very different spaces: Red Square, Alexander Garden and the Kremlin Riverfront. Previously, these spaces were autonomous and reserved for governmental representation. The purpose of the project is to design engaged spaces which are open for a broader public. All three spaces form a pedestrian ring through which one can circumnavigate the old core of the city. Each space is redesigned by using some formal feature from its rich tradition, but on the other hand, they all provide spaces for contemporary activities.

Figure 2.8
Igor Marjanović, B.Arch. Diploma Portfolio, Moscow Architectural Institute (together with Uros Vuković and Marija Milinković), an example of an urban design project with site plan as combination of image and text

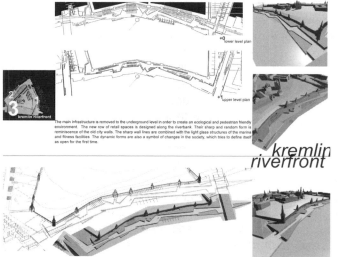

Figure 2.9
Igor Marjanović, The B.Arch. Diploma Portfolio, Moscow Architectural Institute (together with Uros Vuković and Marija Milinković), boards as combination of traditional drawings and 3D models

your portfolio here will include large-scale drawings, even regional maps. Igor Marjanović's portfolio (see Figures 2.8 and 2.9) deals with urban design issues, while demonstrating some of the theoretical background of the project through use of quotations. It also combines large-scale maps and drawings with 3D computer renderings to emphasize the scale at which ideas can be pursued.

Landscape Urbanism, Contemporary Urbanism and Urban Design References

Chung, Chuihua Judy (Ed.); Inaba, Jeffrey; Koolhaas, Rem; Leong, Sze Tsung. Great Leap Forward: Harvard Design School Project on the City. New York: Taschen America Llc., 2002

Chung, Chuihua Judy (Ed.); Inaba, Jeffrey; Koolhaas, Rem; Leong, Sze Tsung. Harvard Design School Guide to Shopping: Harvard Design School Project on the City 2. New York: Taschen America Llc., 2002

Corner, James; MacLean, Alex (Photographer); Van Valkenburgh, Michael (Introduction). Taking Measures Across the American Landscape. New Haven: Yale University Press, 1996

Daskalakis, Georgia; Waldheim, Charles; Young, Jason (Eds). Stalking Detroit. Barcelona: Actar Editorial, 2001

Koolhaas, Rem; Mau, Bruce; Siegler, Jennifer (Ed.). S, M, L, XL. New York: The Monacelli Press, 1996

Moughtin, J. C., *et al.* Urban Design Methods and Techniques. Oxford: Architectural Press, 1999

Landscape Urbanism, Contemporary Urbanism and Urban Design Practices

Field Operations, Stan Allen and James Corner, Principals, New York City, USA. Website: NA

MVRDV, Winy Maas, Jacob van Rijs, Nathalie de Vries, Principals, Rotterdam, The Netherlands. Website: http://www.mvrdv.archined.nl/

OMA (Office for Metropolitan Architecture), Rem Koolhaas, Principal, Rotterdam, The Netherlands and New York City, USA

West 8, Adriaan Geuze, Principal, Rotterdam, The Netherlands. Website: http://www.west8.nl

Sustainable or Green Architecture

Sustainable Architecture is closely linked to various ecological and 'green' movements and deals with the use of ecologically sustainable materials, methods of construction, and programmes. It also deals with energy efficient modes of construction. It has obvious overlaps with landscape urbanism, but has a much longer history and body of research, and generally operates at a smaller scale. Green Architecture can include the use of recycled materials and energy conservation to lead to designs with little or no dependence on non-renewable energy. Some of the schools that have this specialization are the Architectural Association (UK), the Bartlett School (UK), Kingston University (UK), Oxford Brookes (UK), the University of North London (UK), and the University of California at Berkeley (USA), If you wish to enter this field, your portfolio may include not only design projects, but also exploration of materials, and you may try to make your portfolio entirely from recycled materials.

Sustainable Architecture References
Berge, Bjorn. Ecology of Building Materials. Oxford: Architectural
    Press, 2001
Centre for Alternative Technology, Machynlleth, Powys, Wales, UK,
    http://www.cat.org.uk
Hagan, Susannah. Taking Shape: A New Contract Between
    Architecture and Nature. Oxford: Architectural Press, 2001
Richardson, Kenneth (ed.). Green Shift: Changing Attitudes in
    Architecture to the Natural World. Oxford: Architectural Press, 1999

Sustainable Architecture Practices
TR Hamzah, Yeang, Ken Yeang, Principal, Kuala Lumpur, Malaysia.
    Website: http://www.trhamzah-yeang.com/
Various international sustainable practices can be found on the
    following website: http://www.ecosustainable.com.au/links.htm#1

Fabrication and Installation

Fabrication deals with the production of architectural objects at one-to-one scale level. These objects offer the experience of architecture at a real scale, not through drawings or models, and very often they are a part of museum installations and exhibitions. Fabrication can often be done through the use of digital technologies, both to produce drawings and to produce objects. Fabrication practices often do designs for museums and public spaces, and are very similar to art practices that focus on public art. This kind of practice provides excellent opportunities for presenting ideas to both architectural and non-architectural audiences. Many young architectural firms begin with fabrications and installations, and later make the transition to more traditional architectural projects. Many schools have studios or units that emphasize this way of working. If you wish to enter this specialization your portfolio may be a physically complex construction and contain photographs showing work at full scale.

Fabrication and Installations References
Costa, Xavier; Riley, Terence; Robbins, Mark; Betsky, Aaron. Fabrications /Fabricaciones. Barcelona: Actar, 1998
Diller, Elizabeth; Scofidio, Ricardo. Flesh: Architectural Probes: The Mutant Body of Architecture. New York: Princeton Architectural Press, 1995

Fabrication and Installations Practices
Dilller and Scofidio, Elizabeth Diller and Ricardo Scofidio, Principals, New York, USA. Website: http://www.dillerscofidio.com/
F.A.T. Fashion, Architecture, Taste, Charles Holland, Sam Jacob, Sean Griffiths, Principals, London, UK. Website: http://www.fat.co.uk/
Muf Architecture/Art, Katherine Clarke and Liza Fior, Principals, London, UK. Website: http://www.muf.co.uk/

Community Architecture

Community Architecture looks for ways of integrating the user and various community groups into the design process. Through not-for-profit organizations, community work brings together architects, users, urban planners and policymakers, politicians, and social workers. The design process often involves design charettes or workshops, where community representatives collaborate with architects and architecture students to generate feasibility studies and sometimes fully developed designs. Schools that offer this specialization are the University of North London (UK), The Rural Studio, Auburn University (USA), McGill University, Montreal (Canada), and the University of Illinois at Chicago (USA). If you wish to enter this specialization, your portfolio should show understanding of, and an interest in, urban or rural policy, patterns of social mobility in the city, the architectural and urban identities of different communities and so on. Your portfolio may have a higher percentage of photographs, reports and interviews.

Community Architecture References
Day, Christopher; Parnell, Rosie. Consensus Design. Oxford: Architectural Press, 2002

Sanoff, Henry. Community Participation Methods in Design and
Planning. New York: John Wiley and Sons, 1999
Wates, Nick. The Community Planning Handbook: How People Can
Shape Their Cities, Towns and Villages in Any Part of the World.
London: Earthscan Publications, Ltd., 2000

Community Architecture Practices
City Design Center, University of Illinois at Chicago, USA. Website:
http://www.uic.edu/aa/cdc/
The Rural Studio, Auburn University, Alabama, USA. Website:
http://www.arch.auburn.edu/ruralstudio/
The Prince's Foundation, London, UK. Website: http://www.princes-
foundation.org/

How to Get There

Once you are familiar with some of the possibilities to practice and
study architecture, you should start tailoring your portfolio so that it
meets the institution's or office's requirements. This means that you
have to understand all of the technical requirements of the application
process, and it also means than you have to be aware of that institution's sensibility, aesthetic ideology, and its position in the market. This
book will examine two procedures that almost always require portfolio
review: applying to a (post) graduate school of architecture, and applying to work in an architectural firm or at a university.

Some aspects of portfolio preparation apply to both procedures,
but some are very different. We will discuss those differences in
Chapters 3, 4, and 5. Wherever you apply, make sure that you
thoroughly research the application process. Call and ask the
selected institutions to mail you all publications, bulletins, and
prospecti they have available. Look at their website, and find out
all about the admission process. Most websites will list a contact
person whom you may call and ask questions, so if you are still not
sure exactly what is needed, call and find out. Try to find out who
will be reviewing your application, how it will be reviewed and
where, and most importantly ask questions about what kind of
portfolio format is expected. Do they require a specific size? Does
the portfolio have a minimum page requirement? Do they want a
slide-based portfolio? Do they accept digital portfolios? If yes, then
ask what kind of digital portfolio is accepted: CD Rom, website, or
something else.

It is most likely that your application will be just one of many – the admission committee might be reviewing thirty applications in a single session. Having that in mind, try to make your portfolio stand out from the crowd, instead of simply following the conventions. Use only the best work available, and try to capture the reviewer's imagination with your work, and by using colour and layout well.

> **As you will put a lot of time, effort, and money in preparing your portfolio, always double check whether or not you will be able to retrieve it. If an institution keeps all portfolios for its records, then check if good quality copies or prints would be acceptable. And remember to always keep a 'back-up' copy of your portfolio and CV with you – you never know when and how quickly you might need one! This kind of careful research will help you begin to understand differences between school and offices, so you can produce the right kind of portfolio for the design culture you are trying to enter.**

3 Design Cultures

This chapter will help explain why there are different design cultures in different schools of architecture and offices. It will introduce the idea that there are different – though often related – aesthetic, theoretical and professional communities within the discipline of architecture, which have different ways of valuing visual, textual and three-dimensional communication. It will also suggest that some of these design cultures are sometimes perceived to be more powerful and influential than others, so that some architectural aesthetics, theories and practices receive greater attention and recognition. This information should help you not only to understand why certain schools or practices are harder to get into than others but, more importantly, it should help you establish an independent and informed assessment of the cultural values of your work. If you understand the value of your work in different cultural contexts, then you should be able to make more appropriate choices about the form and content of your portfolio so as to (hopefully) end up where you want to be.

Cultural Capital and You

Before we explain various design cultures and markets, you might want to become familiar with a new term: cultural capital. In his writings, the French sociologist and philosopher Pierre Bourdieu focuses on the role of education in the eventual social roles that different people end up having. He invents a term, cultural capital, for the kind of value that people acquire as a result of their educational experience, as well as other kinds of cultural history. Understanding cultural capital and how it is created and maintained may help you to decide the relative importance of conventional success in your personal and professional life, and may help you to understand how your portfolio may be received and understood in different situations.

For Bourdieu, culture and education are fought over by competing groups, each struggling to possess, retain and increase their cultural influence. He believes that in order to get and keep cultural influence you have to have high cultural capital – the intellectual and creative 'luggage' you carry with you. Your cultural capital is most clearly evident in your résumé or CV, but your portfolio also plays a part. Because it contains the cultural objects you have made, your portfolio becomes a kind of cultural bank. The kinds of projects you have done, with and for whom, and especially what they look like, will affect your cultural capital. The more your work resembles that of the most prestigious architecture schools or offices, the greater the chances of you joining them and being successful. This may sound pretty awful but it is generally true. Occasionally, unusual students do cross these boundaries, but it is important to remember that in order to achieve this your portfolio will have to be triply beautiful and clear, making you outstanding in a unique way.

> **Cultural capital is not about money – it is about value and influence. It is about where you went to school, who your professors were, where and for whom you worked, and how important your projects were. As well as being about your work, it is about your network of friends, employers, teachers, clients, and colleagues. The more important or influential your work and networks are, the greater the likelihood of your success. Architecture school can help you forge both work and networks – going to schools with high reputations can therefore be worth all the money you or your parents spend on your tuition and fees.**

Cultural capital can also be about the cultural objects you own – from a painting to a car, although that is unlikely to impact on your portfolio or interview. Finally, cultural capital can also be about who you are, what you look like, how you dress, speak, move, smell, how you cut your hair or look at people. That part of cultural capital is beyond the scope of this book, but think about this as you prepare for your interview. Try to visit the school or office, and see how people dress and talk. In particular, in architectural offices you will be evaluated on your personal character and attributes (employers cite this as the first thing they look for) so make sure that you have made a conscious decision as to how you want to look and be perceived. If you do not like the look of an office culture (everyone wearing suits whilst you like to hang out in jeans) it is likely you will not be offered a position.

Being aware of how cultural capital is measured might help you to put together a more successful portfolio or résumé, and prepare for an interview, or it may help you decide that you do not care for that kind of measurement at all. Not having much cultural capital is fine if you know what you want to do, where you can do it, the people who do it, and how to find a way to join them. Whichever way you decide to go, you should know that the 'playing field' is not always 'level' and that different cultures may have different cultural capital in different contexts. The architectural profession still has many prejudices – roughly only just over 10 per cent of the profession is female, and black/African American architects form only 1 per cent of the profession, both in the USA and the UK. Architecture schools are more liberal and reflective of the real percentages of women and minorities in the total population. A good book to read is American Architects and the Mechanics of Fame, by Roxanne Kuter Williamson, University of Texas Press, which shows that most of America's famous (white male) architects were either educated by, or worked for, a small 'family' of other famous (white male) architects.

If you are interested in your portfolio being seen as having cultural capital, it is important that you look at work that has already had a high level of recognition – competition winning designs, designs that have won student awards, and so on. It is also important to know how to present your work graphically and verbally – again you can get clues from other good architects' works and from the way good architects talk about their work. It is also important that you believe in your portfolio and invest the kind of time and money in it that reflects that belief. If you do not believe in it, then it will be harder for others to do so. However, being over-bombastic, both visually and verbally, actually diminishes its value – the best kind of cultural capital is the one that appears natural and this means not having to brag. If you genuinely doubt the value of some of your work, then you should not overstate your case but instead discuss and evaluate it with someone you respect before you complete your portfolio – your professor or a practising architect. Help them help you see the strong points in your work, your portfolio, and yourself.

You should also quietly and firmly emphasize and maintain the importance of those people that you studied or worked with, who are included on your résumé. In a quiet, unobtrusive way, include their names in your portfolio. If some of your professors are famous designers or thinkers make sure that in your résumé and portfolio you indicate that you took their class. If you worked for a firm that won national design awards mention it in your résumé and include some of the projects in which you played a part in your portfolio. Try to formulate your previous experience in a way that proves your excellence and uniqueness, and your capacity to associate with people who are seen as high achievers in your field. Talk to your previous professors and bosses and ask them for any contacts they have that might be helpful. Also, if you are sure that some of them are 'heavy on cultural capital' and it is important to you to emphasize this, then make sure to ask them for the letter of recommendation. If you want to know more about how cultural capital works in a specific situation, see 'Curriculum Vitae – The Architect's Cultural Capital: Educational Practices and Financial Investments' in Hill, J. (ed.), Occupying Architecture, London and New York: Routledge, pp. 23–37.

It is important to realise that cultural capital is usually gained through education and one's association with various institutions (universities, firms, professional associations and the like) as well as association with important individuals. Your choice of school will affect some of your future life directions, networks of friends, professional associates, and so on. By understanding how architectural institutions operate, you will be able to join the ones that represent your hopes and ambitions so that you can do work that is interesting and meaningful, and can use the available resources and systems of professional networking to eventually turn projects into reality.

Academic Markets

Schools of architecture vary enormously in their theoretical, formal and professional identities, and of course in their cultural capital. Understanding these cultural differences will make it more likely that you will find the right school for you. Always research the academic programme you are applying for – carefully review all materials sent you by the school, look at their website, find out what the faculty research interests are, what kind of work they produce and think about how you can fit in that environment.

Some schools publish their students' work on an annual basis so use those publications to understand the aesthetic and theoretical position of the school. These publications include the AA Files (Architectural Association, London, UK), the Bartlett Book of Ideas

(Bartlett School of Architecture, University College London, UK), Hunch (The Berlage Institute, Rotterdam, The Netherlands), Harvard Design Review (Harvard University, Cambridge, USA), The Education of an Architect (Cooper Union, New York, USA) etc. You can buy

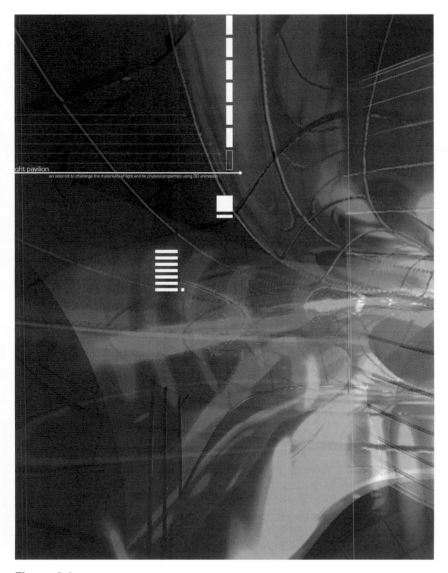

Figure 3.1
Christopher Ciraulo, Light Pavilion

these and other publications directly from the schools or in most architectural bookstores such as the Triangle Bookstore at the Architectural Association, London, The RIBA Bookstore at the Royal Institute of British Architects, London, and the Prairie Avenue Bookstore, Chicago, USA. Most are also available from on-line booksellers, so research before you buy, since some are expensive. Some of the portfolio examples from this chapter show close links to contemporary architectural aesthetics which rely on the use of digital media (see Figures 3.1 and 3.2) and work well on-line.

Most importantly, remember that professional success is not only about what you know, but WHO you know! Talk to your professors, alumni and friends and see if there is a connection between them and the school you are trying to enter. In particular, ask your professors if they know someone at your dream school or office. See if a professor you know is well respected there and if so, ask for a letter of recommendation from him or her. If a professor really thinks you are a good student, and feels there is a potential strong match between you and the school, he or she may even be willing to make a phone call and therefore create an introduction for you.

If he or she is not willing (many professors feel that is going too far), find out if there are any former students from your current school

Figure 3.2
Zane Karpova, Shi-ga Museum, contextual montages, Schiff Award 2002, SOM Travelling Fellowship 2002

at your prospective school/office, and get in touch. They will not only be a mine of useful information, but may give you good advice about the admissions process, in particular about the portfolio. After all, they were successfully admitted themselves. Use your existing networks, make new ones, and do not be afraid to ask. Professors at your current school may be keen to help – their own cultural capital can increase if you become successful.

The best way to understand a school is to visit it. Many schools have Open Houses and Year-End Shows where you can see the work they do and meet the Graduate Programme Director, faculty, and students. Try sitting in on their reviews and lecture classes, as you will get a much more accurate picture. Talk to as many people as possible, ask them about the strengths of the programme, and their plans for the future. Students are usually the most sincere advisers – they will tell you the truth! If you are interested in studying with someone in particular always check if that person will be teaching in the year you will be studying, as some professors might be on sabbatical leave to conduct research, or may be in the process of leaving to go to another school. Find out what kind of work that person does so that you can make sure you have work in your portfolio that is close to his or her interests.

Selecting the right programme is one of the most important decisions you will make in your early career. Keep in mind that the quality or specialization of the programme might determine your professional future. Although college rankings are neither completely accurate nor absolutely true, it is useful to check them. Some good resources for checking rankings of architectural programmes in the USA include the US News and the Design Almanac website. The former is generally based on academic parameters, while the latter is based on professional parameters, i.e. how well schools place their graduates into practice. Keep in mind that some interesting schools or colleges might not be well known or highly ranked, but might have a programme that suits your interests, like the Rural Studio at Auburn University, Alabama, or the Boston Architectural Center, USA, or the Prince of Wales Institute, London, UK. Some programmes may not be very good overall, but may have a curriculum concentration that might be just what you are looking for.

Rural Studio website: http://www.arch.auburn.edu/ruralstudio/
Boston Architectural Center website:
   http://www.the-bac.edu/home.html
Prince of Wales Institute website:
   http://www.princes-foundation.org/

Professional Markets – How Do You Know This is The Place for You?

Applying for a job in an architectural office also requires extensive research about professional markets. Think carefully about what kind of work you would like to do, where would you like to do it, and then define the most appropriate strategy to get the position. Many firms have websites, and that is the best place to start. Look at projects, see if you would be happy working on them, and whether you have skills that would make you attractive to that office. If you are looking to work in a large firm, websites will also give you a contact name from the Human Resources Department whom you can call and ask questions about the application process, as firms might have special application forms and special portfolio requirements with regard to format and content. Some firms also publish annual journals, like the SOM Journal in the USA, or might have a monograph on their design work. Look for those publications in the bookstores and on the web, and see if your portfolio can complement their area of expertise. If a firm does not have a website, call anyway, and ask them to send you their publicity brochure or practice portfolio, or copies of publications about their work. Some one or two-person practices may not have any of these forms of publicity so you will simply have to apply 'blind' and use the interview process to see if there is a match.

Do not dismiss a firm because it does not have good publicity materials. Some firms work with long-standing clients, and may not need publicity. However, a firm with no publicity or publications may make it harder for you to get the cultural capital you may need later to get into larger, more prominent firms. If you do not have much choice about where you end up working (this happens all the time, particularly in an economic recession), and find yourself in a firm with little interest in creating and maintaining their own publicity, take the initiative and document your work yourself as beautifully as you can. Often the firm will be grateful for your extra effort.

> **It is important to remember that the firm owns the copyright of the work it produces, even if you did the design and all the drawings, so you can only use the documentation for your personal portfolio.**

Different offices have different cultures and systems of values. Architectural firms vary in size and types of works they do. Some offices have more than three-hundred employees, while other can have less than ten. Would you like to be a part of a large corporate environment or are you more comfortable in a smaller setting? Do you prefer to work on large-scale projects or would you like to get hands-on experience on a building site? Large offices can offer you a range of projects, typically big in scale, and they might also give you an opportunity to work on various projects around the world. Some of them have a dress code (i.e. no jeans, etc.) and might be more formal than others. Sometimes these offices might be divided into studios, which cover different market or building types. Smaller firms can give you an opportunity to be involved in a range of building types and construction administration. Therefore, do not dismiss a firm because it is small. Often you can get the best experience in a small firm, because you will do a little (or a lot!) of everything. Do not dismiss large firms either. You may end up doing projects overseas, get to know leading consultants, and be able to specialize in some unusual areas.

Some of the largest architectural firms are:

- Arup Associates: www.arupassociates.com
- Foster and Partners: www.fosterandpartners.com
- Gensler – Architecture, Design and Planning Worldwide: http://www.gensler.com

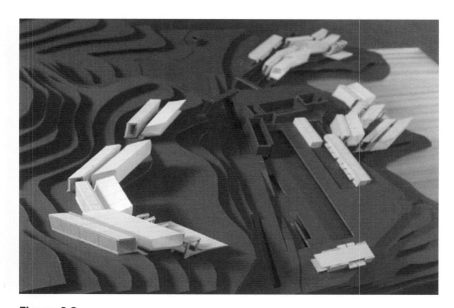

Figure 3.3
Zane Karpova, Shi-ga Museum, study model photos

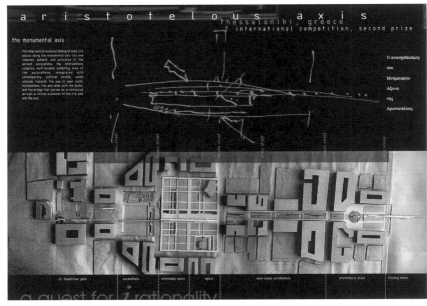

Figure 3.4
Ivan Subanović, Aristotelous Axis, Thessalonica, Greece, International
Competition, second prize (together with Milan Maksimović, Karolina
Damjanović, Zorica Petković)

* O'Donnell, Wicklund, Pigozzi and Petersen Inc.: www.owpp.com
* Richard Rogers Partnership: www.richardrogers.co.uk
* Skidmore Owings and Merrill LLP: Architecture, Engineering,
  Planning, Interior Design, Graphics, Project Management:
  www.som.com

As a practising architect you can be involved in a variety of projects
and different firms might specialize in certain aspects of architectural
practice. You can practice architecture in a design-oriented firm whose
range of expertise includes architecture, interiors and planning. Larger
engineering companies often employ architects, so if you are a structures whizzkid consider this as an option. You might also consider
working for a graphic design firm, especially if your strength is in web
design. Architects can also be employed by various government
agencies, such as municipalities, departments of buildings, park
districts, etc. You can also be involved with various community groups
and non-profit agencies. Architects are also increasingly involved in
design build, real estate and contracting, so think about working for a

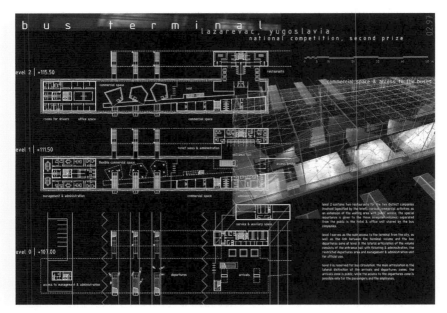

Figure 3.5
Ivan Subanović, Bus Terminal, Lazarevac, Serbia, National Design
Competition, second prize (together with Milan Maksimović, Maja Kusmuk,
Zorica Petković)

contractor or a project management company. Some architects are
involved in less traditional design work, such as art installations or
public art, and are employed in artists' studios. You should be aware
of these possibilities before you make your choice – it is possible to
switch disciplines and move from one to another. Each areas of
practice requires a different emphasis in the portfolio. Tailor your
portfolio so that it fits the specific market you want to join, and understand that market by looking at the work and how it communicates
visually, verbally, physically and digitally where appropriate. Ivan
Subanovic's portfolio (M.Arch, Architectural Association, London) and
Clare Lyster's portfolios (M.Arch, Yale University) demonstrate strong
interest in built forms and therefore are very physical with exceptional
use of beautifully crafted architectural forms (see figures 3.5–3.8).

International Cultures

Perhaps the most difficult differences to understand are the international ones. By the time you have been at architecture school for

The professional architect...

A hard shell that fits all the softtoys

"What I'm leading up to is that out of this unconscious, out of this deeper self, out of this portion of ourselves of which we generally are afraid and therefore try to keep under control, out of this comes the ability to play—to enjoy, to fantasy, to laugh, to loaf, to be spontaneous—and, what's more important for us here, creativity, which is a kind of intellectual play, which is a kind of permission to be ourselves, to fantasy, to let loose, and to be crazy, privately. [...] And what does threaten us is softness, fantasy, emotional 'childishness'".

E.H. Maslow

Figure 3.6
Marjan Colletti. The Professional Architect, M.Arch design work at the Bartlett School of Architecture, London, UK, montage of drawings, photos and text

URBAN COCKTAIL

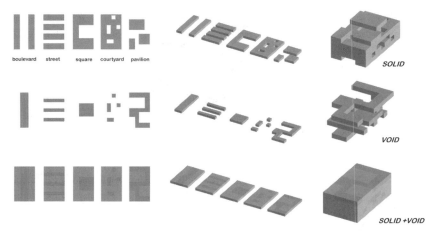

Figure 3.7
Clare Lyster, Monaghan, 3D volumetric studies

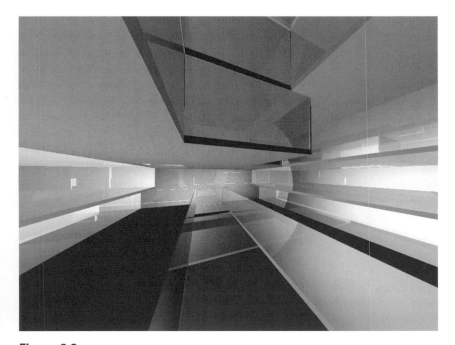

Figure 3.8
Clare Lyster, Monaghan, digital interior perspective

a couple of years, you will have talked to enough professors and students to know something about architectural education and practice in your own region or country. Some of your professors will also be well-informed about architectural schools and firms abroad, but their knowledge will necessarily be incomplete. Sometimes their information may also be out-of-date, as schools and firms change with the people who run them and work in them. There may also be big regional differences in architectural culture, even in smaller countries like the UK. If you live in a country where access to the Internet is difficult or expensive, you may find it harder to get up-to-date information on schools and firms. If you are thinking of making an international move, your research will be even more crucial in preparing you for the changes in design cultures you will encounter. You will certainly need to adapt in ways that you have not foreseen, improving not only your verbal language skills, but having to gain new visual, technical, theoretical and professional skills. Your portfolio should suggest your capacity to adapt and integrate some of the design and professional culture of your chosen destination in your work. By highlighting your ability to work in diverse cultures and professional contexts, you will open many doors to different professional markets and therefore might be less dependent on the economy of one place. RED's portfolio for example (see Figures 3.9 and 3.10) includes design work for Beirut, although this small practice is actually based in London.

United Kingdom

The Architects Registration Board (ARB) website section on careers lists all validated schools of architecture in the UK, with their website and e-mail addresses. The Royal Institute of British Architects (RIBA) website section on the President's Medals has portfolios of winning students from many UK as well as some international schools of architecture. The winning portfolios (Bronze and Silver Medal winners) will give you an idea of the kind of work recognized as outstanding in the UK in recent years. However, UK schools vary enormously in their design cultures, so if you work or your ambitions do not fit what you see at first, keep looking.

If you are an EU student

Having decided where you want to apply, trying to enter British architectural education as an international student involves different

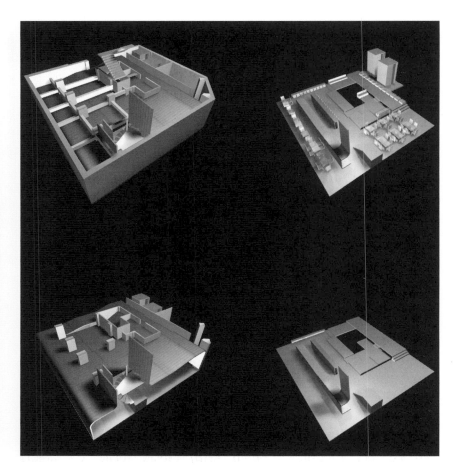

Figure 3.9
RED (A. Ramirez and D. Stojanović), 3D layers

Figure 3.10
RED (A. Ramirez and D. Stojanović), Project for Beirut

processes, depending on the country in which you live and which stage of architectural education you have already completed. If you are a resident of the European Union you will find there is an agreement in place to allow you credit for study you have already undertaken and therefore your portfolio will usually be the main focus of the school's evaluation. Your fees should also be the same as that for a British student, but do check with the school to which you are applying as legislation can change.

If you are a foreign student

If you are resident outside the European Economic Area (EEA, currently consisting of the European Union – Austria, Belgium, Denmark, Finland, France, Germany, Greece, Ireland, Italy, Luxemburg, the Netherlands, Portugal, Spain and Sweden – and Iceland, Liechtenstein and Norway) you will normally be called an overseas student and pay higher fees. There is very little financial assistance for overseas students studying in the UK – you will have to be outstanding to get any help, and the competition will be intense. Schools will probably not tell you that these higher fees may make you financially more attractive, but they may tell you if they have limits on the number of overseas students they can recruit. Do not be embarrassed to ask about any constraints on overseas recruitment.

The second factor that adds importance to your portfolio will be the stage of completion of your architectural education. You should make the level of your completed education absolutely clear in your portfolio and résumé. Like UK or EEA students, as an international student your application will be considered differently at undergraduate and postgraduate level. If you have never studied architecture before and are applying to enter an undergraduate programme you may or may not need to submit a portfolio or attend an interview, so find out whether there are specific requirements. If you are applying for a postgraduate programme you will almost certainly need a portfolio, and may be asked to attend an interview as well. If this is difficult or expensive, do not be daunted. Some schools may allow you to send them the portfolio and offer you a telephone interview. Others may accept or reject you on the basis of the portfolio alone. In the latter case, your portfolio becomes even more important so you should be prepared.

Apart from differential fees, there will be another difference between you and the EEA applicant. You will most likely need an undergraduate degree from a school validated by the joint ARB/RIBA validation

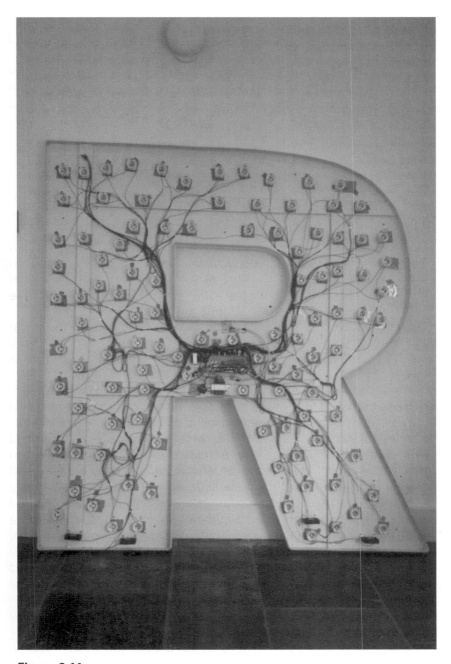

Figure 3.11
Mark Chalmers, R, architectural installation

board as the majority of UK schools make this a basic requirement for entry to postgraduate education. Do check with each school, your own school, and the ARB and RIBA for the most up-to-date information. The new school will also be able to advise you what, if anything, you can do if the school where you studied is not validated by ARB/RIBA. Some schools will accept students into earlier years and this may be useful if you can afford the additional fees. UKCOSA is a good source of information for international students, providing information about immigration, financial assistance and so on, but it focuses on all international students and will not be able to provide a specifically architectural perspective.

Resources:

- ARB website: http://www.arb.org.uk
- RIBA website: http://www.architecture.com
- UKCOSA website: http://www.ukcosa.org.uk

Europe

European schools cover a huge range of teaching approaches, so making a decision about applications and portfolios will need a lot of research. Pan-European architectural institutions are still young, but with the advance of European integration processes they are gaining more significance. The European Association for Architectural Education (EAAE) is an international, non-profit organization, founded in 1975, that promotes the exchange of ideas and people within the field of architectural education and research. The Association respects the pedagogical and administrative approaches of the different schools and countries. It has two official languages: French and English. The EAAE organizes conferences, workshops, summer schools. There are also regional associations, like the Architectural Council of Central and Eastern Europe (ACCEE). Some national architectural institutions (similar to the RIBA) can also be a very good source of information on architectural education and practice. The Netherlands Architecture Institute (NAi) for example, has a very extensive website, with a broad range of information about the Dutch and international architectural scene. Some European countries, like Germany and Spain, make completion and passing of the diploma examination equivalent to passing the licencing/registration exam. This can make the diploma portfolio from those countries more technical in emphasis, with a broader range of technical drawings and information, and can lead to more consistent formal approaches within

each school. Remember this as you make your portfolio for competition in the European marketplace and play to your strengths.
Resources:

* EAAE (AEEA) website: http://www.eaae.be/eaae/
* NAi website: www.nai.nl
* UIA website: www.uia-architectes.org

USA and Canada

The architectural profession in North America is administered by several institutions, and each can be an excellent source of information in its own area. The American Institute of Architects (AIA) is the largest professional architectural organization on the continent. The AIA has local chapters, which can be a useful source of information about architectural opportunities. For example, the AIA Chicago Chapter has an extensive website with numerous job and learning opportunities in the Chicago area.

The National Council of Architectural Registration Boards (NCARB) is a non-profit federation of fifty-five architectural registration boards in the United States, and controls professional standards as well as the licensing of architects. The Council manages a number of services for interns and architects. The Intern Development Programme (IDP) defines levels of training in architectural practice related to the architectural licensing exam. Through the IDP mentorship system, architectural interns and recent graduates get advice and guidance from practitioners, maintaining an IDP record documenting their internship activities and hours spent working on schematic design, design development, construction administration, etc. If you are an intern (year-out student), the IDP categories will help you identify the kind of documents you need to have in your portfolio to show you have had the broadest experience possible. You do not, however, need a portfolio to pass IDP requirements. NCARB also manages the Architect Record Examination (ARE) that is necessary for licensure. It tests candidates for their knowledge, skills and ability to provide the various services required in the design and construction of buildings. A portfolio is not required to pass the ARE.

The National Architectural Accrediting Board (NAAB) is the only organization authorized to accredit USA professional degree programmes in architecture. Most state registration boards in the United States require applicants for licensure to be graduates of NAAB-accredited programmes, making those programmes an essential aspect of preparing for the professional practice of architecture. Accredited programmes are expected to substantially meet standards that the NAAB has defined as appropriate education for an architect. Currently, there are two types of NAAB accredited professional degrees in the USA: the five-year undergraduate Bachelor of Architecture degree, and the two to three-and-a-half year Master of Architecture (for precise terminology please go to the NAAB website). It is important for international students to know that the one-year post-professional Master of Architecture degree is not accredited by the NAAB and, therefore, completion of such a degree alone will not allow you to get licensed in the USA. Each school is required by the NAAB to be very clear about which degrees are accredited. As you can imagine, competition for the accredited degrees can be much greater than for non-accredited degrees, although places in one-year post-professional masters' degrees in the top schools are also very hotly contested. A portfolio for entry to an accredited degree will need to have a lot more information, as the admissions committee will be checking whether you not only have the kind of work that fits the culture of the school, but will be checking that you have completed courses that meet its degree prerequisites, including the GRE exams and TOEFL tests where appropriate.

The Association of Collegiate Schools of Architecture (ACSA) is a nonprofit, membership association with 250 schools in several membership categories, quite a few outside the USA. The ACSA website has an excellent section on architectural education, high school preparation, architectural programmes, how to select a school, and architectural practice. It is geared mainly for students resident in the USA, but much of its information is useful to international appli-cants too. Its resources page provides useful links to other websites, especially to its member schools, and also to information about USA architectural education and practice. Use it to help you find out about different schools or architecture.

Finally, the American educational system has a long tradition of student organizations. Some of them, specifically related to archi-tecture, include the National Organization of Minority Architecture Students (NOMAS), and the American Institute of Architecture Students (AIAS). AIAS organizes students to advance the art and science of architecture. It is also a student voice in the decision-making process of organizations such as the American Institute of Architects (AIA), Association of Collegiate Schools of Architecture (ACSA), and National Architectural Accrediting Board (NAAB). NOMAS has local chapters in most major American urban architecture schools as well

as historically black schools of architecture and currently represents African-American, Latino, Asian-American and other minority groups in architecture.
Resources:

- AIA website: http://www.aia.org/
- AIAS website: http://www.aiasnatl.org/
- AIA Chicago Chapter website: http://www.aiachicago.org/
- NCARB website: http://www.ncarb.org/
- NAAB website: http://www.naab.org/
- ACSA: website: http://www.acsa-arch.org/
- NOMAS website: http://www.noma.net/student_chapters.htm

South America

South American practising architects, educators, and students have various institutions that regulate the architectural profession on their continent. National organizations in South America are very strong. The Institute of Architects of Brazil (IAB) is one of the largest organizations on the continent, and it administers competitions, national conferences, and other events. The professional institute for architects in Argentina is Consejo Profesional de Arquitectura y Urbanismo (CPAU). CPAU has an extensive website, which offers information about architectural practice in Argentina. Please note that most of professional sites and educational programmes in South America are either in Spanish (Argentina, Chile, etc.) or in Portuguese (Brazil), which means that it is very hard to study and practice architecture in South America without the basic language skills. South America is also the location of two very important architectural and art exhibitions: the Buenos Aires and São Paolo Biennales. Schools of architecture and their websites and publications can be a good source of information about professional activities and markets in South America.
Resources:

- Consejo Profesional de Arquitectura y Urbanismo (CPAU) website: http://www.cpau.org/
- Institute of Architects of Brazil (Instituto De Arquitetos Do Brasil – IAB): http://www.iab.org.br/
- Faculdade de Arquitetura e Urbanismo da Universidade de São Paulo (FAUUSP) website: http://www.usp.br/fau/
- Facultad de Arquitectura, Diseño y Urbanismo Universidad De Buenos Aires website: http://www.fadu.uba.ar/homepage.html

Africa

Architectural education in sub-Saharan Africa in the past forty years has been most heavily influenced by the colonial legacy in the continents' respective countries and the changes or needs brought about by independence. The three most dominant models of education (British, French, Portuguese) have been modified or adapted post-independence whilst schools in the north of the continent reflect their Islamic and North African cultural heritage. For English-speaking institutions there is a trend towards seeking validation from two bodies, the Royal Institute of British Architects and the Commonwealth Institute of Architects, with internal professional bodies often partnering with RIBA to produce joint validation criteria (as in the case of the South African Institute of Architects, for example). The move towards a more global system of validation (across the continent or in partnership with RIBA/CIA) is seen as a positive one which will encourage wider access and cross-cultural participation and make it easier for students to move between institutions in the West and at home.

The curricula of many of the post-independence schools reflects the demands of countries in the developing world: in many of the English-speaking countries, architectural education tends towards stronger engineering and science-based models and the department of architecture is most commonly found as part of a larger engineering faculty (KNUST in Kumasi, Ghana, or University of Lagos, for example) although there have been recent moves to form closer allegiance with art departments in many countries which have strong arts or humanities faculties, or to link with planning and urban studies (UCT, Cape Town and University of Witwatersrand, Johannesburg) to form faculties of the built environment. In general, students from African schools wishing to apply to universities overseas should be prepared to include evidence of art-based and more conceptual work as the curricula of many schools in Europe, North America and Asia tends to lean towards the latter.

The internet has had a dramatic impact in terms of access to information and discourses surrounding architecture and education. In places where publications have historically been out of reach, both financially and in terms of very weak distribution infrastructure, students are now able to keep abreast of developments and dialogue both at home and abroad. Use of the computer in many schools in sub-Saharan Africa is now routine: in terms of portfolio submissions, this technology is already being widely used although server speeds and reliability vary.

In terms of publications and domestic architectural culture, South Africa has the most developed internal infrastructure with numerous publications, website, international exhibitions and events, etc. Some useful sites to visit are:

- South African Institute of Architects website: http://saia.org.za
- D_ezine website: http://www.dezine.co.za
- Penrose Press website: penrose-press.com/IDD/edu/Africa.html

Asia, The Indian sub-continent And The Middle East

In Asia and the Indian sub-continent design cultures have been changing rapidly in the last five years. Whilst RIBA and, to a lesser extent, AIA and UNESCO were for a long time the international validation bodies for middle-Eastern and Asian schools, more recently Asian schools in particular have begun to coordinate their own educational agendas. Organizations like ARCASIA (Architects Regional Council of Asia) and ACAE (ARCASIA's Committee on Architectural Education) have formed to share ideas about architecture, architectural education and architectural practice. ARCASIA is a council consisting of the Presidents of National Institutes of Architects in the Asian region who are members of the organization. Annual meetings are held in different member institute countries, to deliberate and to give collective directions and representation to matters that affect the architectural profession in the Asian region. The Architectureasia website lists the websites of many of the architectural schools in the Indian subcontinent and the Far East.

China has a small number of architecture schools for its population, and entry is therefore very competitive. Graduates of these schools are outstanding and compete very well in the international marketplace. Hong Kong has several schools of architecture, including the University of Hong Kong, the Chinese University of Hong Kong, and Hong Kong Polytechnic. Here too, graduates can be outstanding.

In the Middle East change has been less sustained, but longstanding traditions of architectural education exist at institutions like the Technical University of Istanbul (Turkey), the American University in Beirut (Lebanon), and the Technion School of Architecture in Israel, and programmes of growing strength in oil-producing states like Saudi Arabia.

Finally, there are some very strong schools of architecture in Australia, including RMIT (the Royal Melbourne Institute of Technology), the University of Sidney and the Curtin University of

Technology in Perth. The Association of Collegiate Schools of Architecture (ACSA) has a large membership that includes not only all USA and Canadian architecture schools, but also many schools around the world. Its website is an excellent resource for contact details for many international schools:

- ACSA (Association of Collegiate Schools of Architecture) Website: http://www.acsa-arch.org
- ARCASIA (Architects Regional Council of Asia) Website: http://www.arcasia.org/
- ACAE (ARCASIA's Committee on Architectural Education) Website: http://www.arch.nus.edu.sg/acae/acae.html, link also available through:
- National University of Singapore Website: http://www.arch.nus.edu.sg/index.html
- Architectureasia Website: http://www.architectureasia.com/

For students wishing to apply to schools of architecture in Europe, North America and South East Asia, the internet is probably the most useful place to start with the RIBA website (http://www.architecture.com) providing the most comprehensive listing of schools and useful sites. Major global schools now have comprehensive sites that often display student work from which prospective students can glean useful information in terms of the school's culture.

A Word of Caution

Finally, depressing though it may sound, prepare for some rejection. There are still significant cultural differences between architectural schools across the world. Access to theoretical and technical knowledge, as well as practical experience associated with advanced development, is easier in some parts of the world. Many schools are aware of this and take it into account when assessing portfolios, recognizing individual creative potential. Most schools also have thoughtful teachers who know there will be a period of adjustment for them and for those international students that are admitted. Really thoughtful teachers welcome the perspectives of international students, ensuring a two-way dialogue between your design culture and theirs. Nevertheless, it is possible that you will encounter a school that does not value your design culture and your application may be rejected. If rejection makes you aware of this difference, and you are still determined to enter that school, you may need to reapply and re-present your work. Try to get feedback about what was missing, and rework the portfolio. The work still needs to be 'yours' but you may need to adjust its emphasis so that the school of your dreams can recognize your potential to learn from and contribute to its design culture. If you are confused, get advice from your professors or fellow students who have had recent international educational experience. Remember that home students may experience this problem too, as there are regional and local cultural differences, as well as differences based on educational background, class, ethnicity and so on. These may be so subtle that neither you nor your audience may understand just exactly what is going on so do not take this situation personally. Adjust your work, or look for a school where you see a closer match. Learn about different architectural cultures. Becoming aware of differ-ences and finding a way to celebrate and accommodate them is one of the fascinating challenges of the international student, educator and architect.

4 Academic Portfolio

In this chapter we will discuss the contents of the academic portfolio in greater detail. The form and content of the portfolio will vary depending on your level of education, what kind of programme or course you are applying for, and whether you are applying for a teaching position.

The Portfolio in the Academy

United Kingdom

Architectural education in the UK is divided into three parts: the undergraduate degree, the graduate degree and the final professional examination. Completion of the undergraduate degree also means taking and passing the first part – called RIBA, Part I – of the professional examination that eventually leads to professional registration as an architect (licensure and registration in the USA). In almost all cases, completion of the postgraduate (equivalent of graduate in the USA) degree also means taking and passing Part II of the professional examination. Part III – the final professional examination – is taken after several years of appropriate professional experience (equivalent to IDP – intern development program – in the USA). Academic environments in the UK (as with most other countries) vary from school to school, and depending on the programme, might have various emphases: design, construction, or management. Matthew Springett's portfolio, for example (see Figures 4.1–4.4), won The RIBA Silver Medal and was produced during his studies at the Bartlett School of Architecture, University College London. It shows the

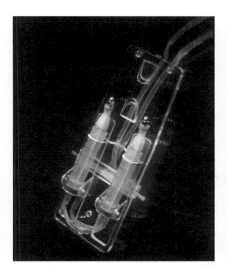

Figure 4.1
Matthew Springett, Manhattan Pig
Farm - model, diploma portfolio,
The Bartlett School of Architecture
1997/98, London, UK, The RIBA
Silver Medal Winner 1998

Figure 4.2
Matthew Springett, Manhattan Pig
Farm, model

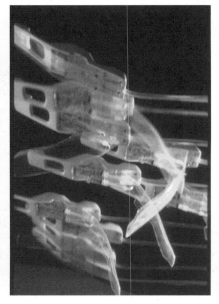

Figure 4.3
Matthew Springett, Manhattan Pig
Farm, model

Figure 4.4
Matthew Springett, Manhattan Pig
Farm, model

Bartlett's emphasis on critical design inquiry, while also demonstrating Matthew's exceptional design skills and ability to produce beautifully crafted work.

Applying to enter a degree or Part I course in the UK often, but not always, requires a portfolio. If an undergraduate degree application requires a portfolio it often means it is more art oriented, as other schools may place more emphasis on 'A' Level or GCSE scores to select their candidates. If you know that your architectural interests have more artistic aspects, then making a strong portfolio will help get you into one of these schools. If, on the other hand, you are more of a liberal humanist, you may not wish to invest energy in a portfolio at this stage. Applying to enter a Part II course in the UK almost always involves submitting a portfolio and, if selected, often involves a personal interview. Here it is really important to do a good job, as the best schools are very hard to enter, and the portfolio could be the deciding factor.

Applying to take the Part III course does not usually involve submitting a portfolio; instead, proof of having taken and passed Part II is generally sufficient. It may be possible to take the Part III examination without having taken and passed Parts I and II, but this involves obtaining an equivalent qualification for these studies and demonstrating appropriate professional experience, both of which involve some significant complications. The ARB and the RIBA would be able to provide more information about this.

The portfolio for entry to a Part I course will vary from school to school but generally the contents need to reflect your creativity, inquisitiveness, spatial understanding, and so on. The portfolio for entry to a Part II course will need to focus almost exclusively on architectural projects completed as a student, and a judicious selection of work from the year out (intern year). It is really important that you call the schools to which you are applying, and find out whether they have specific requirements and deadlines. Do not try to bend rules here, especially with deadlines, as many schools have to make recommendations for admission to their upper administrations to timelines that they may not be able to change.

The Part III portfolio will vary from school to school, and can include essays, a case study or simply passing a written examination. External applicants not affiliated to a school who take the Part III examination (frequently overseas architects seeking registration in the UK) will need to have a professional as well as an educational portfolio and should seek the advice of the ARB and the RIBA regarding its contents.

Applications for teaching positions in the UK, particularly if the position involves studio teaching, usually require a portfolio of work. Here, depending on the design culture of the school, it may be advisable to include not only the work you did as a student, as well as your own professional work, but also the work of your students where possible, along with syllabi, documentation of exhibitions of student work, and so on. Informal enquiries about portfolio traditions will be most helpful, as most schools do not have guidelines for portfolios related to applications for teaching positions. It is also generally a good idea to show versatility in a UK teaching portfolio. Unlike the USA, where positions are usually advertised as already specialized (at most combining design and one other area), in the UK in some schools teaching can involve the integration of design, technology, theory, and professional practice. It is crucial to check with the school what kind of candidate they are seeking.

United States

Generally speaking, architectural education in the USA is divided into two systems: the five-year professional undergraduate degree; and the four-plus-two degree consisting or a four-year pre-professional undergraduate Bachelor of Arts or Sciences degree and a two- or two-and-a-half graduate Master of Architecture degree.

The five-year system is the older of the two, and gives priority to architectural subjects rather than a broad range of liberal arts or sciences subjects. If you enrol, do not like the programme after a few years, and leave, you leave with no qualification at all. The four-plus-two system is more recent, and is based on the professional education of other professions, such as law. In the undergraduate component, architectural subjects are balanced with liberal arts or science subjects. Therefore, if you find you do not want to continue onto the graduate professional degree, you still graduate with a degree, which is attractive in a number of related areas including design, construction management, landscape architecture, engineering and so on. The professional degree (B.Arch., or M.Arch.) makes you eligible for an architectural licensing exam, while a pre-professional degree in architecture means that in the majority of USA states you cannot get licensed with that degree alone.

In order to get into any graduate school in the USA, you will have to submit a portfolio. Even undergraduate programs can sometimes require a portfolio review. A typical application package will include the portfolio, application form, letters of recommendation, statement of intent and your official school transcripts sent directly to the Registrar's office. Some schools might handle applications differently, so it is always a good idea to call and verify exactly what you have to submit. Based on your grades and your portfolio, you might also get various kinds of financial aid, including scholarships. It is not an exaggeration if we say that your portfolio is the single most important part of your application package. With your portfolio, you want to demonstrate your design, technical, and theoretical abilities.

Most schools are centered on design, so make sure that your portfolio speaks about your design excellence, but also make sure that your ideas are clear. Backed by adequate or excellent transcripts, your outstanding portfolio will open many doors for you. Figures 4.5 and 4.6 show Chris Ciraulo's portfolio prepared for application to Graduate Studies in the USA, while Figures 4.7 and 4.8 show Jeff Morgan's graduate portfolio from the University of Illinois at Chicago. In both cases, strong but simple graphics are complemented by computer renderings and many conceptual sketches and diagrams that explain the development of design ideas. Keep in mind that it is not enough

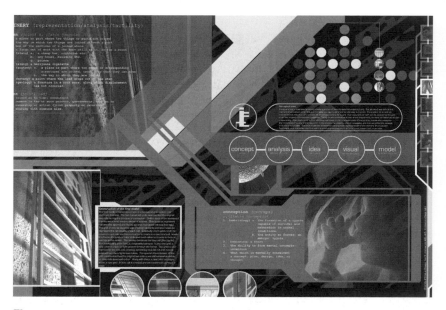

Figure 4.5
Christopher Ciraulo, undergraduate coursework at the University of Illinois at Chicago, demonstrating consistency of the academic narrative from the first concept to the final model

to include just the final design schemes in your portfolio. Most admission committees will appreciate seeing the chronology and development of your design ideas and your ability to carry those ideas through various stages of the design process.

The Academic Narrative

Entering a Programme

Your academic portfolio will need to consist of edited documents that present a specific message or messages for an audience or audiences consisting of one or more professors at the school to which you are applying. Even if you are applying to get into the first year of an undergraduate degree, you should already have visual and/or written material that you can edit or re-format to construct a particular impression you want to give to the school. Whichever the level of your application, before you begin editing and reformatting, you should find out as much as you can about the school where you want to send the portfolio. Go

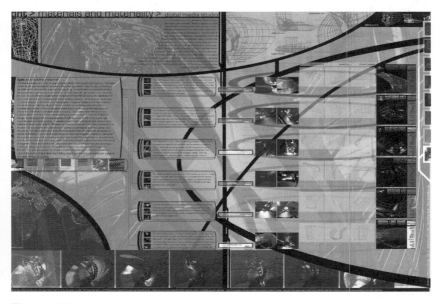

Figure 4.6
Christopher Ciraulo, Digital Media concentration coursework; text and diagrams are used to explain ideas and to support the narrative

intermodal train station: mendrisio, switzerland

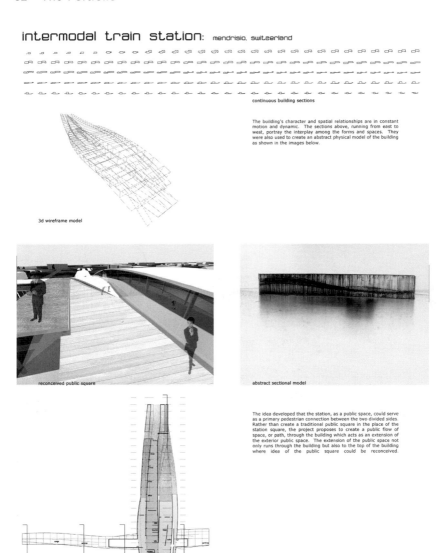

continuous building sections

The building's character and spatial relationships are in constant motion and dynamic. The sections above, running from east to west, portray the interplay among the forms and spaces. They were also used to create an abstract physical model of the building as shown in the images below.

3d wireframe model

reconceived public square

abstract sectional model

The idea developed that the station, as a public space, could serve as a primary pedestrian connection between the two divided sides. Rather than create a traditional public square in the place of the station square, the project proposes to create a public flow of space, or path, through the building which acts as an extension of the exterior public space. The extension of the public space not only runs through the building but also to the top of the building where idea of the public square could be reconceived.

plan illustrating station cargo and landscape

Figure 4.7
Jeffrey Morgan, Intermodal Train Station, Mendrisio, Switzerland, development of design ideas shown through diagrams, wire-frame models, montages, and architectural plans and sections

intermodal train station: mendrisio. switzerland

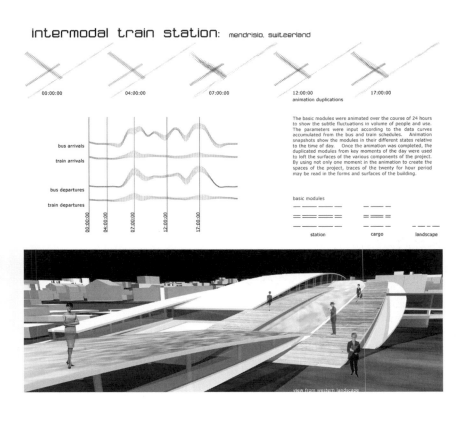

00:00:00   04:00:00   07:00:00   12:00:00   17:00:00
animation duplications

bus arrivals

train arrivals

bus departures

train departures

The basic modules were animated over the course of 24 hours to show the subtle fluctuations in volume of people and use. The parameters were input according to the data curves accumulated from the bus and train schedules. Animation snapshots show the modules in their different states relative to the time of day. Once the animation was completed, the duplicated modules from key moments of the day were used to loft the surfaces of the various components of the project. By using not only one moment in the animation to create the spaces of the project, traces of the twenty four hour period may be read in the forms and surfaces of the building.

basic modules

station   cargo   landscape

view from western landscape

Currently, this stranded zone is a "heterogeneous fabric" that has largely been ignored by the historic city center of Mendrisio. However, the fact remains that the railway acts as a physical barrier between the two areas of the city. Therefore, one of the issues the project addresses is how to minimize or mitigate the effects of the railway to allow and encourage both visitors and inhabitants of Mendrisio to experience the entire city. In order to support such interaction between the two parts of the city, it is necessary to create more than just physical linkages. Perhaps more essential to the development of this zone is the inclusion of program that attracts people to the area, not only for recreation, business, or commerce, but also for living.

The phrase "In Between" has multiple layers of meaning specific to the project site for Mendrisio. At a much larger scale, Mendrisio lies between two major metropolitan areas of Zurich and Milan. At the scale of the city of Mendrisio, the railway has constructed a barrier between the historic town center and the area immediately west of the tracks. Finally, within the specific boundaries of the site, the project attempts to mediate between existing areas of articulated program.

Figure 4.8
Jeffrey Morgan, Intermodal Train Station, Mendrisio, Switzerland

to its web site, and find out what the school's values are, what kind of work the students and professors do, whether it has a technical emphasis, a theoretical one, and so on. Even more importantly, if you can, go to its Year-End-Show or Open House, look at the work and talk to students. Find out if you get excited about the work of the school – if you are not, it is probably a bad idea to apply in the first place. If you like what you hear and see, then find out, if you can, the underlying ideas in the portfolios of some of the students who were admitted. If you see a connection between your ideas and those of the school, arrange your work to highlight the connection. In almost all schools of architecture the admissions tutor or committee will be looking for evidence of creativity, strong ideas, increased sophistication in ideas, and execution of work over time. With postgraduate application portfolios, schools will need to see a growing demonstration of competence in a wide range of areas, from visual communication to writing and some hands-on three-dimensional work. In most instances, this will mean you will need to construct an academic narrative involving a chronology – whether a chronology of ideas, projects, or experience.

Passing a Year/Programme

In the UK it is more important to show a progression of ideas as your final year undergraduate or graduate portfolio may be evaluated on two years' worth of work, although your final project will usually be the most important one. It is normal to begin the portfolio with your earliest work, and end with your latest.

In the USA, where your grade points average will determine whether you pass or fail a degree, you will more likely be evaluated on a portfolio of work only if you are being considered for prizes or a scholarship. In this situation there is usually more scope to change the order of the projects to show your best side – many schools prefer to see the last work first and you can often omit a really disastrous project, edit out all but the best drawings, and even reformat a project for the review. Whichever the case, you must check with your school which format it prefers.

In countries like Germany or Spain where you become licensed upon graduation, you will be evaluated mainly on your thesis or Diploma project, and will need a comprehensive set of drawings. It is helpful to the professors evaluating your work to see that you have prepared and tested a set of ideas, have found a sophisticated set of planning, architectural and design solutions as appropriate, and have represented the resulting building or design in the clearest way possible. Using words to help you explain your progress is very useful, but check with your professors just how much language you need, as there are some schools that prefer the drawings to speak for themselves as much as possible.

Academic CV, References, and Statement of Intent

Initially, you should check with a school about the admission requirements. A typical application package in the UK or USA consists of a statement of intent, curriculum vitae (CV), three letters of recommendations and a portfolio. Call the programme coordinator and confirm what the precise application components are, where you should send the material and for whose attention. Some additional materials might be required, such as transcripts or degree certificates, so contact the admission office to make sure you have everything. Use only reliable carriers for sending out your application – the last thing you want is a lost application package! Ask for delivery confirmation, and in addition to that call the school to confirm that it has received your package in good condition.

> **When writing your application, always use spell check, and have someone look at your writing. The whole package should demonstrate your academic excellence in which there is no room for errors in spelling and grammar.**

Academic Curriculum Vitae

Applying for Graduate or Postgraduate Study

The Curriculum Vitae, usually called 'CV', is your academic and professional biography. The CV is typically used in academia. It is much longer than a résumé – which is also biographical, but is only an outline – and is typically used to apply for a job in an office. There are some standards which need to be adhered to when it comes to writing a CV. First and foremost, list your full name, contact address, telephone, fax number and e-mail address, in case someone needs to contact you. Then list Universities and Schools attended and degrees received. Describe your degree as precisely as it appears on your diploma, because this will affect the length of your Graduate Studies (B.Sc., B.Arch, B.A., etc.) and even the scholarships that may be available. Check the precise wording of your degree with your previous school – this may seem bureaucratic to you, but if it makes a difference in the time and money you will need to study, it becomes very important indeed.

Then describe your professional experience, with exact names of your employers, your job titles, and responsibilities. You can also briefly describe the projects on which you worked (building type, site, square footage, client, site, etc.). Sometimes your professional experience might be in fields other than architecture. List that experience too, but highlight those aspects that make you useful to the school or simply highlight the responsibilities and skills you acquired (management of time, people, goods, supervision, communication skills, etc.). List all academic and professional honours, awards, prizes, and scholarships. Also, list all relevant skills, especially computer skills and familiarity with various types of software.

Carefully examine everything you did and try to put it in your CV. Have a professor or adviser look at your CV – you will be amazed how many things you may have left out. Some schools have workshops or career days, and some of those might have CV writing workshops. Make sure that your CV is easy to read and navigate; text should be well-spaced with the font size no smaller than 10 points. Graphics should be clean and understandable. Use bold and italic letters to highlight the most important achievements. Use good quality paper and make sure that the print quality is superb. You must demonstrate that you are always diligent and detail-oriented, no matter what kind of work you are doing. If you are really into graphic design, you can design your CV, portfolio, and a letter of intent in a similar manner (i.e. use the same font, colour, type of paper, etc.). Overall your CV should be easy to read, well-spaced, and attractive.

Academic References and Letters of Recommendation

References are another important part of your application. Check with the school about what kind of references they need. Do they need letters of recommendations only from your previous instructors, or do they want a combination of academic and professional recommendations? Most schools have very specific requirements when it comes to letters of recommendation and you should be able to find out about those requirements either on the web site, or in the graduate programme prospectus. If you cannot find written guidelines, call the school's office and ask them directly. They will most probably want the letters sent directly from referees to the school office. Some

Figure 4.9
Dr Jose Gamez, Principal Investigator and Jeff Hartnett, Co-Investigator, Las Vegas Research Project, academic research project used for a teaching position application showing the contemporary application of the ideas of Robert Venturi and Denise Scott-Brown

schools might even have specific forms for recommendations that can be downloaded from the web. Typically, each letter must have a full name, title, affiliation and referee contact details, in case the school wants to touch base with them to verify your credentials.

> **Be strategic when selecting your referees. Try to select someone who is very familiar with your work and can write enthusiastically on your behalf. It is very important to make the letter as personal as possible, instead of just using general descriptions of your abilities. Give a copy of your CV to each reviewer as that will refresh their memory about your work and academic achievements. Again, pay attention to their cultural capital, and try to find someone who is well known or at least known in the institution you are applying to. Find out whether a referee might be willing to make a follow-up call on your behalf. Although this is not typical, it might be extremely helpful.**

Academic Statement of Intent

The Statement of Intent should be well-written, eloquent, enthusiastic, and optimistic. It should demonstrate your desire to expand your design knowledge through design research, experimentation, and various forms of inquiries. Try to keep it short, no more than one to two pages long. As with your CV, always use spell check and have someone look at your grammar and writing. Check with the admissions office if there are special requirements in regard to the format. Similar to your CV, it should be well spaced, with the font size no smaller than 10 points, and printed on good quality paper. Demonstrate your motivation to further your education, and explain why you are interested in that particular school. Without saying it literally, explain how you can be a good match for the programme. If you are applying for several places at the same time, do NOT send the same letter everywhere. You can recycle some parts of the text, but each letter should be targeted to a specific school and its programme. Try to find out the school's philosophy, its mission statement and its strengths. If you are applying to a programme in a different country, then explain why you are doing so and what you are hoping to get out of it. Mention your main achievements and honours, especially if they fit the school to which you are applying. Do not be afraid to be personal, as the interviewers will not only be looking for your achievements and interests, but also for your passion and commitment to the subject.

5 Professional Portfolio

In this chapter we will discuss the professional portfolio as a part of an application package for a professional position in an architectural office. The professional portfolio, like the academic portfolio, can take different formats depending on the office in which you would like to work, the country in which it is located, which stage of the application/interview process you find yourself, and what level of responsibility you are seeking.

The Portfolio in the Workplace

The portfolio in the workplace is part of a bigger application package. There are four elements of an application for a position in an office: a cover letter, a résumé, an initial portfolio and an interview portfolio. Each of these parts of your application needs to be attractive and focused, as well as easy to read and handle. Architectural offices, especially the well-known ones, sometimes process hundreds of applications a month, so your work and credentials need not only to stand out, but also avoid frustrating the person who is looking at your package. Each part of the application package needs to be simple for another reason: unless you have existing strengths in a niche area, or there is a shortage of architectural employees (this can happen in an economic boom but is rarer that you might think), or have researched the offices to whom you are applying and you know there is a good match between you, it is entirely possible that you will be sending out a hundred job applications or more. Making a complex portfolio and résumé will make it very expensive for you to copy and mail each package.

Whether or not you send out a large number of applications 'on spec', research about a particular office, like research about a school, is essential, as it will help you, at the very least, to adjust your cover letter, and highlight certain aspects of your résumé and portfolio. Form letters will only tell the office that you are not really interested in working for them. Call each office before you apply, ask to speak to the person who selects candidates for interview, and enquire about the kind of application materials he or she will want to see, as well as when and how they are reviewed. This kind of research will show that you are serious about your application, and will give you a much better idea of how to adjust your application to suit the office. If you get no return call, do not despair – in an economic recession this can be common as offices will be far less likely to have vacancies, and may well have cut employees. Interviewers will be stretched thin, doing not only additional work for the office, but handling bigger volumes of applications. Do not, however, give up either – call again until you learn that there is either no job or, hopefully, hear better news. Persistence may lead you to be offered an interview, even if there is no work at the time. It is not that unusual for an interview to lead to a job offer later on – offices can keep details of outstanding candidates for some time and call back when work comes in (make sure that if you move, you pass on your new contact details – particularly easy to forget if you are finishing either your undergraduate or graduate degree). Or, you may call on just the day that the office has received a significant commission and needs help, so stay optimistic. At the same time it is very important to grow a thick skin to handle the rejections and to keep going.

The Professional Narrative

The initial portfolio you attach with your application – the application portfolio – is the principal means of attracting the attention of the office and getting selected for interview. As with the academic portfolio, you should focus on what kind of a message this portfolio is trying to convey. What are the strengths of your work as a student and as a professional? How can you show your usefulness to this office succinctly in a four- to eight-page format? What evidence or promise of practical competence does your work show? Can you show a translation of design ideas into built work? How can your résumé help to support the application portfolio's contents? Can you find a related graphic layout, and can you include key elements from the résumé in twenty seconds before they accept or reject your application? As with any architectural competition, the impression you make in the first ten seconds is the most important. Figures 5.1 and 5.2 are taken from the portfolios of Clare Lyster and Rahman Polk, and although they are using different visual vocabularies and aesthetics, these two portfolios each communicate their ideas clearly. Strong graphics, with black background, highlight the complexity of built forms, while the text clarifies some of the design intentions that might not be obvious from the computer renderings.

Once you are invited to interview, it is even more important to research what kind of fuller portfolio and supporting information you will need to bring to the interview. Your interview portfolio will play a big, though not the only, part of the interview process. Find out, by calling the office, who will be doing the interviewing, and whether you will be interviewed by one person or by a group. Try to find out as much as you can about the interviewer/s, as well as about the work and values of the office – go to the office website, and ask your friends or professors whether they know the interviewer, or anyone who works at that office. If they know others at the office, call them and try to learn as much as you can, especially what kind of candidate they are looking for. For example, if you have worked in sustainable design, and the office is looking for someone in that area, you will need to highlight that work in your portfolio. If you have worked on a set of construction drawings, check whether the office has a particular interest in seeing the whole project, will want to see the drawing set in full, and whether it is acceptable to reduce it in size. Different offices have different preferences about this – some interviewers may get impatient looking at a large sheaf of drawings, whereas others will see it as essential. It will probably be less important to the interviewer to see how your work has developed and more important to see what range of skills it covers. It is therefore less likely to have a chronological narrative than your academic portfolio, although this may vary with different offices.

Having said this, it is likely that the work you will have done at school or for another professional employer will not belong to the same world of ideas as the office that is interviewing you. Surveys of architectural employers have shown that your ability to communicate, adapt and fit in to the culture of an office are the most important evaluation categories in an interview. Your cultural capital in that instance will only partly consist of your portfolio. More important will be the cultural capital you demonstrate through your appearance and behaviour. An office knows that you will need to learn how that office works

this portfolio to aid the linkage? Can you do something very simple to tailor each portfolio, at least in part, to the focus of the particular office? How can you use colour, layout, text, drawings and photos to capture the imagination of the person who may only have ten or

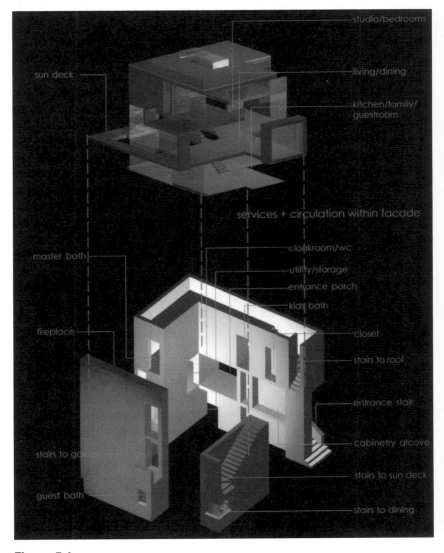

Figure 5.1
Clare Lyster, Tower House, 3D diagrams showing building envelope and interest in physical aspects of architectural design

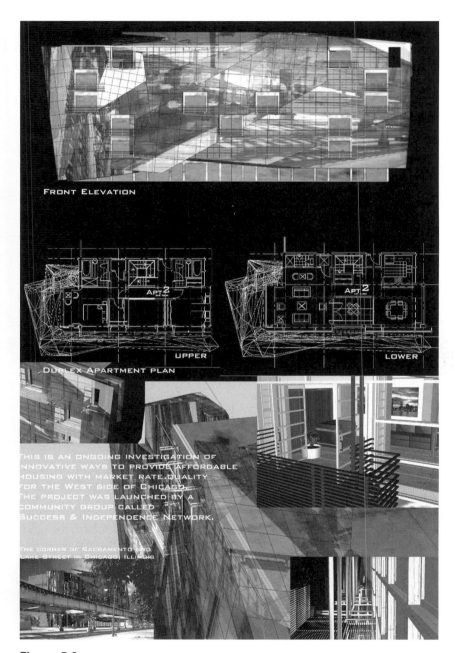

Figure 5.2
Rahman Polk, Success and Independence Network, combination of plans, elevation, renderings and text

– and that to do this you will need to be a team player, to speak with clarity and confidence while demonstrating humility about your ideas, to show a willingness to listen, change and to learn, to care about your own competence, to have respect for others, to have a sense of humour, to be ethical, to show commitment to a project and to work hard to turn it into reality – in short, that you can act as a professional. You can help demonstrate that you can do all this in the way that you talk about your work at the interview, so you should make sure that you have some visual and verbal elements in the portfolio to remind you to do so. Unlike the educational portfolio, where you can be more eccentric, the professional 'narrative' is generally as much about your qualities as a person that will fit the office culture as it is about your work.

There are, of course, offices that do not fit this stereotype. If you do not fit this stereotype either, you need to find out where these offices are, how they deal with applicants, what kind of portfolios they like, how they interview and so on.

Finally, you and your work may be so individualistic or so eccentric that you/it will not fit into any of the architectural office cultures you initially encounter. If this is the case, see if you and your work will fit

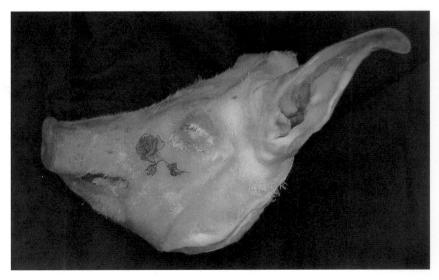

Figure 5.3
Mark Chalmers, The Pig, diploma portfolio, Kingston University, London, UK, shock effect used to explore cultural aspects of skin markings as drawing

into related disciplines, or think about starting your own business, and how your portfolio may become a part of that strategy. Mark Chalmers graduated from Kingston University, UK and his portfolio (Figures 5.3 and 5.4), demonstrates cross-disciplinary interest in graphic art design, corporate identity and interior architecture. On the other hand, Katrin Klingenberg's portfolio contains a flyer with a collage of diverse services that her small practice offers. Wherever your final destination, you will still need to have a portfolio that communicates your talents and skills to an audience that you think is looking for them, and that means researching that market.

The Professional Résumé, References and Cover Letter

Your application package should begin with the cover letter, followed by your résumé (including names of your references) and finally include a mini-portfolio.

Your cover letter should be short and clear, stating who you are, for which position you are applying, why you are applying, and why you hope you will be able to make a positive contribution to the office.

Figure 5.4
Mark Chalmers, The Disney Store, design practice combining architecture and corporate identity

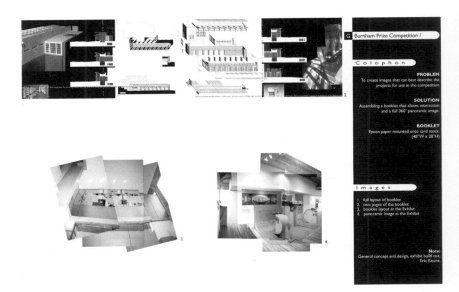

Figure 5.5
Anthony Max D. Marty, Burnham Prize Competition, layering of structural
elements and textual explanations of the concept

It should have clear contact details – your address, phone number,
e-mail address, and website url if you have one. It should also be
simple and pleasing to the eye.

Your résumé should also be clear and attractive. It should be no
longer than two pages and be printed on thicker, better quality paper
than the cover letter so that it stands out by weight and quality. It
can include colour if that helps the clarity of the communication
process or makes the kind of visual impression you want to make.
The reason it has to be short is that it is a résumé, not a CV. It is
a summary, whereas a CV is exactly what it says – in Latin: the run
of your life, or your life's achievements. Remember, a bad résumé
can lose you a job – if an office sees you cannot summarize your
strengths easily, it will be concerned about your other communication skills and your ability to focus. Your résumé should show how
the expertise and experience you have is relevant to the position for
which you are interviewing. That may mean having different versions
of the résumé, each emphasizing specific strengths in relation to the
job you want.

Professional Portfolio 77

> **Your résumé must be concise. It should be accurate and truthful, and free of grammar or spelling mistakes. Do not fudge anything, show your strengths and have someone with good English proofread it. It can consist of a narrative or bullet format, or a combination of both. If it has narrative, this should be short and to the point.**

In the United States it is not appropriate to include information (or indeed be asked at interview) about your marital status, your age, or health, as this may be seen as discriminatory so do not put such information on your résumé. Once you are offered the position, your employer may then ask for such information in order to negotiate health insurance, etc. In the UK, however, job application forms often do ask for such information. As with the portfolio, it is important to check for national differences in résumé writing through friends, professors and advisers.

There are certain things that must be included on your résumé. As a minimum they should consist of:

- Your name, address, telephone number, e-mail address and web page url if you have one.
- Your educational qualifications, dates of study, including the date you obtained your qualifications, and where you obtained them. If you won prizes include them in the appropriate time period.
- Your employment experience to date, including the names of your employers, the dates of employment, and a brief summary of the work you did. For example: Project Architect – responsible for

Figure 5.6
Ryan Knock, Warehouse Mixed-use Conversions, CAD perspective and project label

Construction Documents, Construction Administration, Details, Coordination of Structural and MEP Consultants, etc.
- Any other knowledge or experience you have that will help you get the job (for example being fluent in a foreign language if you are applying to an office with much of its work overseas, or community service if you are applying for a job in an office doing community architecture).

In many other employment areas references are not required on the résumé. In architecture, however, it may be as important who you know (that will be able to vouch for your skills and personal characteristics) as what you know, so check with your interviewer how many references he or she requires (three is usual). If you do not list any of your former employers or professors as references, the person reading your résumé may assume that you have something to hide, which is why you need to check. Your last employer is usually the one you should put first on the list of references, as he or she will have most recent knowledge of you. It is VERY important to check with all of your references that they agree to do this for you before you list them. It is possible that some will turn you down. If this is the case, do not be disheartened, and go on to ask the next person.

> **Finally, it is really helpful to re-read your résumé the day before the interview, so that you are ready for questions at the interview. For examples of résumés please go to the website for this book.**

Documenting Built Work

It is very important to document all of your built work. Take slides, photos, or digital photos of your structures. Photos can be used for folios and Powerpoint presentations, while slides might be more suitable for periodicals and traditional slide shows. Be very careful when taking photos of your buildings. Try to capture the best views. These photos should emphasize the strengths of your design and construction abilities. If there are any interesting details on the building, then take close-up shots of these details. If some of the buildings that you have worked on get publicity, try to find any articles published on them and include these in your portfolio. It is extremely important to be precise and accurate about your contribution to the project. A work of architecture is usually a result of team effort and based on

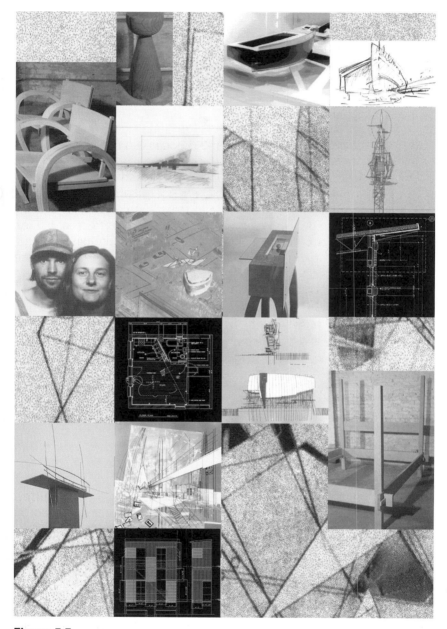

Figure 5.7
Nicholas Smith and Katrin Klingenberg, grid of marketing images –
sketches, drawings, models, design-build, and perspectives – showing the
diversity of their practice

professional collegiality, so define your role and title on the project (designer, member of the design team, project architect, project manager, intern architect or production assistant) and ALWAYS give credit to fellow colleagues. Together with photos of a built structure, you can show some of the most interesting construction drawings, such as plans, wall sections, details, etc.

Like all other parts of your portfolio, this one should be well-thought out and crafted. The best way to assure high quality is to look for examples in architectural periodicals and books. Look at some of the architectural journals and see how they document built work. Try to establish meaningful and visually balanced relationships between the photos and drawings, image and text.

Some journals that you might want to consult are:

- Architectural Record
- Architectural Review
- The Architects Journal
- Detail
- Domus
- L'Architecture D'Aujourdhui

Construction Drawings

Many offices will ask you to demonstrate your ability to produce clean and neat construction drawings. By doing so, you demonstrate understanding of structure, materials, details, and modes of construction. Computerized construction drawings will also demonstrate your ability to use software systems such as AutoCAD, Microstation, ArchiCAD, etc. Try to find out what software is being used in an office and if you are familiar with it make sure to point that out in your CV and portfolio. The American Institute of Architects and the Royal Institute of British Architects define specifically what architectural drawings should be in a typical set of construction documents and how they should be numbered (G1.01 for General Info, A1.01 for the first floor plan, etc.).

If you have a set of construction drawings, take it with you to the interview and discuss it with your interviewer. If you are including construction drawings in your portfolio, try to show the breadth of these (plans, sections, details, opening schedules). This will demonstrate your ability to work on various parts of design process and will also demonstrate your expertise in building technology. Sometimes construction drawings might be jammed with various layers, notes, symbols, tables, blocks, etc. If this is the case, you can enlarge one part of the drawing showing all the layers and then show the whole sheet reduced, just as a reference, or even with some layers turned off. When printing construction drawings, try to print them directly from the software in which they were originally produced, as this will preserve the line quality.

6 Preparing the Portfolio of Work

In this chapter we will concentrate on the system of organization you will need to make sure you prepare your portfolio to represent the broadest range of your talents and skills, to be up-to-date and of course to be beautifully produced and reproduced.

Selecting, Recording, and Storing Your Work

Selecting Work

The first rule of selecting work is 'select only the best'. In other words, only include work that shows your strengths in particular areas, and, within those, shows your breadth. That usually, but not always, means selecting the projects that have had good grades or marks, or have won competitions. However, you may have components of projects that have been unsuccessful as a whole, but may show strengths in an area of which you feel proud. It is not unusual for a graduate admissions tutor or committee to admit a student who has an average undergraduate degree but whose portfolio collates work that is excellent in areas that the new school supports. Whilst an admissions decision like that is still a gamble, it is a calculated one, assuming that the student will flower in an environment where his or her strengths can be nurtured.

The second rule of selecting work is 'select work that communicates quickly and visually'. Portfolio evaluations are usually very fast, both in the educational world and in professional practice. Words should be at the service of the visual message, and simplicity of text is usually most effective. However, if one of your strengths is writing, then in an academic portfolio it can be entirely appropriate to include your best essay. Do not, however, expect it to be read in its entirety; rather, assume that it will be skimmed and certain passages may be

Figure 6.1
Anthony Halawith, Adaptive Restaurant Design, M.Arch thesis project, University of Illinois at Urbana-Champaign, IL, USA

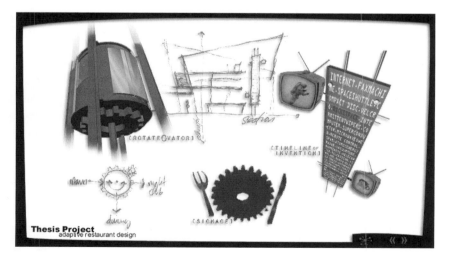

Figure 6.2
Anthony Halawith, M.Arch thesis project

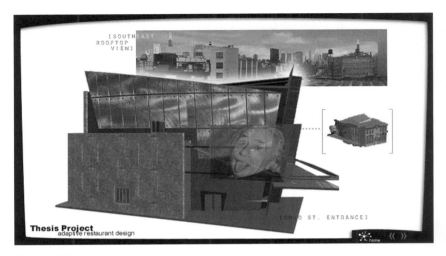

Figure 6.3
Anthony Halawith, M.Arch thesis project

read in greater detail. Never include written work that you know has spelling mistakes or grammatical errors.

Recording Work

The governing principle for recording work is very different to selecting work. Here the rule is 'record/copy everything'. This means that you will need to get organized, making sure you have equipment to do so yourself, or know where you can have it done if you can afford to pay someone else. The main thing to remember is that you need to record work on a regular basis, usually just after a mid-term or final review. Recording your work at those times, when time pressures are usually less great, also allows you to reflect on the work itself, and may help to develop the project, or at least the presentation of its main ideas. It can also give you a sense of achievement.

Depending on the format of the work, make sure you have reprographic copies, digital files and/or photos of your whole portfolio as well as of the individual images that comprise it. This way, if your portfolio should be lost in the mail you can reproduce it. It will also allow you to continue to edit the portfolio and adjust its format for different occasions. Keep the original and edit only the formatted copies, so that you have a record of what you sent to whom. Make sure you have back-ups of digital work in progress, as well as

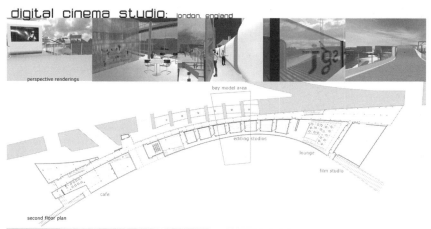

digital cinema studio: london, england

perspective renderings

The cross-section of the building needed to resolve a multitude of issues. Because of the tremendous noise levels under the arches of the viaduct, it was hypothesized that the network servers and mainframe of the facility could be located under them. The editing suites located on the second floor needed maximum acoustic and vibration isolation. Thus, the solid formed spaces were elevated on special absorbing columns to eliminate noise generated through vibration. The interstitial spaces located above and below the first floor provided another opportunity to enhance the elevation dynamic.

To decrease the direct sound transmission from the viaduct to the roof of the building, a steel and glass structure was constructed along the length of the building. In addition to providing some acoustic protection, the surfaces were also available for digital media projections, advertisements and artwork. The structure of the building never comes into contact with the structure of the viaduct, thus creating an open void space between the two. Mechanical and maintenance spaces are located in two lower level rooms at the extreme ends of the facility. a pathway connects the two underground while also accommodating main service runs.

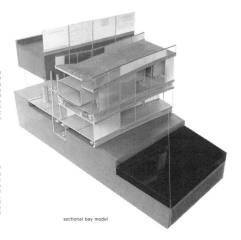

sectional bay model

Figure 6.4
Jeffrey Morgan, Digital Cinema Studio, London, UK, diversity of representation - computer renderings, drawings, photos of the model and text

completed work, and set up a ritual for making back-ups on a regular basis. Make sure you use professional quality photography whenever possible – use your school lab, and borrow professional lighting and cameras if your school does not have such facilities. If you can afford to use professionals then do so – you will no doubt need them later on as your professional career evolves. Finally, get the advice of your professors, especially if they have award-winning work as they will have a lot of technical, compositional and organizational experience that will be helpful.

Storing Work

There are some simple things you can do to make sure your portfolio stays in good shape. First, make sure that you keep a hard copy of the folio in the flat file or plan chest which you bought for your loose work. The flat file should allow the work to stay flat, in the dark, and in dry conditions. This may sound silly, but make sure you have a lock on the flat file and that it is located away from general activity. Later on in life, if you have children and/or pets, you really will need to make sure that 'the dog does not eat the drawings'. Second, remember that digital material gets corrupted in time, so re-copy digital originals every five years. Keep duplicates of both the hard and digital copy of the portfolio. Third, the best way to store models is to hang them on the wall, preferably with a cover. Make covers out of plexi or Perspex, so that your models do not become permanently glued with dust. Finally, when can you destroy your work? The answer is – never. It is a part of your professional history and identity, and you never know when you may return to early work for ideas or for publication.

Scanning, Reducing, and Reproducing Your Work

Scanning your work in an appropriate format and resolution is one of the most important aspects of the portfolio preparation process. For example, most of Matthew Springett's work from the Bartlett School, University College London (Figure 6.5), is done by hand, and therefore it is extremely important to scan this kind of work very carefully, so that the original line quality can be translated into digital format. You can scan your drawings on various types of scanners, depending on the format of your drawings. You can use the most common A4 size scanner (or 'letter size' in the USA), or you can use large scanners if you have bigger boards. Scanners will still provide much better image quality than digital cameras. Most schools have oversize scanners, but if not, commercial reprographic stores can provide you with this service, although this can often be very expensive. If you have slides of your work, you can also scan them through a slide-

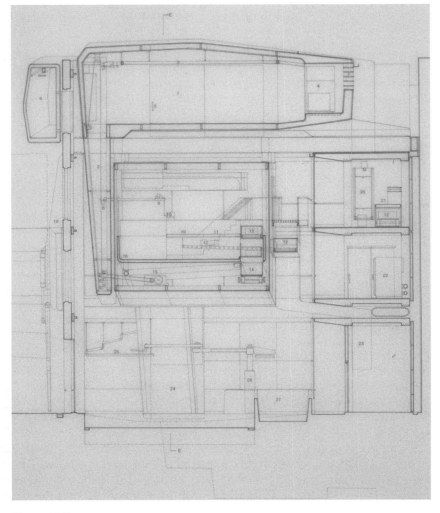

Figure 6.5
Matthew Springett, Manhattan Pig Farm, section, diploma portfolio, The Bartlett School of Architecture 1997/98, London, UK, The RIBA Silver Medal Winner 1998

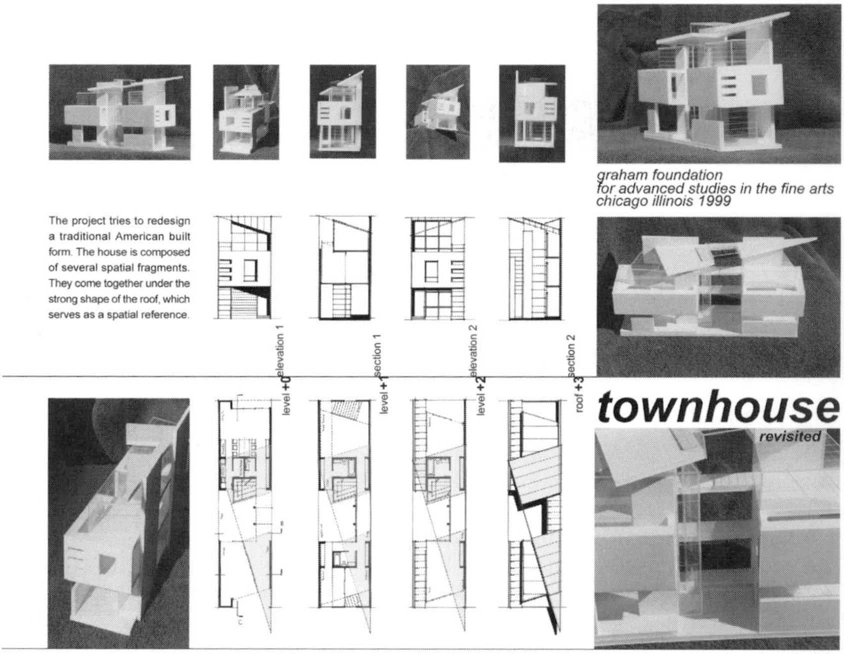
graham foundation
for advanced studies in the fine arts
chicago illinois 1999
The project tries to redesign a traditional American built form. The house is composed of several spatial fragments. They come together under the strong shape of the roof, which serves as a spatial reference.
elevation 1
section 1
elevation 2
section 2
level +0
level +1
level +2
roof +3
townhouse
revisited

Figure 6.6
Igor Marjanović, Chicago Townhouse, combination of traditional drawings and a pattern of low resolution photos of the model

scanning accessory. Some of the images from Igor Marjanović's portfolio for example (see Figures 6.6 and 6.7), are digital images of the physical models or scanned images of 35 mm slides. When you scan slides, scan them in much higher resolution, because it is most likely that you will need them bigger than 35 mm × 35 mm.

Once you start playing with scanned images, you will hear the expression 'dpi' quite often and it is important to understand what it means. DPI (or PPI, pixels per inch) means 'Dot Per Inch' and it tells you how much information is packed into every square inch relative to the image that you scan. It is also often referred to as resolution. All computer monitors see everything at 72 DPI, so if you scan an image at 300 DPI, it will appear larger on the screen than the actual final print size. The resolution of a display monitor is almost always given as a pair of numbers that indicate the screen's width and height in pixels. For example, a monitor may be specified as being 640 × 480, 800 × 600, 1024 × 768, and so on (the first number in the pair

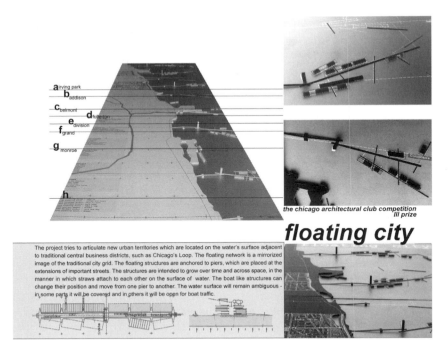

The project tries to articulate new urban territories which are located on the water's surface adjacent to traditional central business districts, such as Chicago's Loop. The floating network is a mirrorized image of the traditional city grid. The floating structures are anchored to piers, which are placed at the extensions of important streets. The structures are intended to grow over time and across space, in the manner in which straws attach to each other on the surface of water. The boat like structures can change their position and move from one pier to another. The water surface will remain ambiguous - in some parts it will be covered and in others it will be open for boat traffic.

the chicago architectural club competition
III prize

floating city

Figure 6.7
Igor Marjanović, Chicago - Floating City, Chicago Architectural Club Design Competition, Third Prize (together with Vuk Vujović), montage of digital photos of the model, traditional drawings and text

is the number of pixels across the screen, and the second number is the number of rows of pixels down the screen).

However, for printing quality purposes you should try to scan all images at 250 dpi. At 250 dpi, you should get 'photo quality' results. It may be worth noting that for professional publishing purposes, the standard is to have images that are a minimum of 300 dpi. If your files get too big, you may reduce the resolution, but do not go below 150 dpi, because your prints will start to be pixilated. The most important thing to understand about image resolution is the relationship between image resolution (dpi/ppi) and image print size (actual width and height). Image resolution and image size (dimensions) are inversely proportional to each other: if you enlarge an image, you lower its resolution. If you reduce an image, you increase its resolution. So, before you even scan an image, make sure that you know the image size required for your portfolio layout. Guess larger if you are uncertain. If the photo is larger than the layout size, simply scan at 300 dpi. Fortunately for those of you who are scanning oversized boards, reduction is not an issue – you can only gain in resolution by reducing the size of your original images.

Two most common image file types are TIFF (Tagged Image File Format) and JPG (Joint Photographers Group). TIFF files tend to retain more information, but JPG files are usually smaller and easier to save and convert. Generally speaking, TIFF files give better printing results, while JPG files are good for displaying on the screen. TIFF uses a lot of 'space' (megabytes) and the difference in quality might not be worth it. For example, a TIFF file at 800 × 600 will take about 1.5 megabytes, whereas a JPG file set to the highest setting will take only about 200 kilobytes. Your eye will not see the difference in quality between the two. The bottom line is: use a JPG, but ensure that you maximize the resolution. For more information on various types of image files, please refer to Chapter 9.

You might also decide to work with photocopiers, which can also give interesting results. As with digital scanning – plan ahead! Make sure you know what the final layout will be, so that you can calculate the exact reduction. Some photocopiers can give you different reductions in X and Y directions. Whichever way you go, make sure you do not lose too much of the original image quality, text definition, and line quality. Out of all of these, the line quality will cause the biggest problem. Whether you draw in AutoCAD or with Rapidograph pens (technical pens), you will discover how difficult it is to preserve the original line quality. If you are converting your AutoCAD files to image files, you might want to work with so-called EPS files, because they tend to preserve the line quality of a linear drawing. If you are scanning hand-drawn boards, you will discover that you cannot reduce them too much, otherwise you will completely lose the original line quality. Instead of reducing, it might be better to scan parts of your boards in high resolution and provide close-ups of your original boards.

7 The Portfolio Container

You never get a second chance to make a first impression, so make sure that your portfolio container absolutely makes the best possible impression. It is precisely the portfolio container – its craft, quality, and creativity – that will create the first impression about your work. This chapter will introduce you to some different options for making a strong first impression through your portfolio container.

Container Quality

You might assume that architects get job offers and commissions purely on the merits of their designs, but the way an architectural portfolio is presented is very telling about your approach to your own work and architectural design in general. Even if your projects are outstanding, original and innovative, a poorly designed and crafted portfolio container suggests that you are not professional, not detail-oriented, and cannot finish the job properly. It is therefore worth spending some time and energy on the portfolio case. Besides making the first impression with its design and visual appearance, your portfolio container should also satisfy some basic technical specifications. Whether you buy the container or you decide to make it yourself, your portfolio container should be water and abrasion-resistant, lightweight yet with sturdy construction. It should also resist puncturing, tearing and moisture.

Buying a Portfolio Container

Buying a portfolio container is usually the quickest way to get your portfolio container, although it still involves a lot of research and shopping around. It can also involve re-printing your work so that it can fit the particular case, which can make the whole process very lengthy. It is also more expensive than making it yourself. Keep in mind that most art stores do NOT accept returns of portfolio cases, so your purchase is very often non-refundable. This is an important parameter for your decision, since most portfolio cases are very expensive. On the other hand, portfolio containers bought in a store or custom made for you will look very professional, clean, and neat. It is generally accepted that financially burdened students cannot afford expensive presentation formats and therefore use simple PVC zip-around binder style carriers, and you will not necessarily be penalized for using this format. However, if you want to make a difference with your portfolio and create a positive impression, you should shop around for some classier and more original alternatives.

Various design-related professionals use a portfolio format in their communication: photographers, graphic designers, fashion designers, etc. Keep in mind that you can buy a portfolio container not only in an architectural store, but also in stores that supply other professional equipment. Typically, you can buy portfolio containers (or portfolio cases) at art stores, office supply stores, regular and university bookstores, and of course you can get them on-line from:

- http://www.portfolios-and-art-cases.com/
- http://www.tranzporter.bizland.com/index.html
- http://www.pearlart.com/
- http://www.utrechtart.com/
- http://www.misterart.com/index.cfm
- http://www.shoptheartstore.com/
- http://www.lgc-unlimited.com (London Graphic Centre)

There are many types of portfolio containers. One of the most common types of portfolio cases is a simple book-style portfolio or a binder with polyethylene sleeves to protect your drawings from fingerprints and other hazards. Although conventional, book-style portfolios are easy to handle, open and display. In a word – they offer a unique ease of use, which sometimes can be very important. Books with refill pages may solve the problem of whether to leave extra pages at the back of the portfolio, until you have enough images to fill the whole book. You can also get custom-made books. London Graphic Centre web site (http://www.lgc-unlimited.com/catalogue/catalog.html) offers a number of stores that can build custom-made book-style portfolios, including those in leather or black-fabric padded covering with concealed brass page fixings and a variety of refill pages, colours, and textures – from traditional leather to modern rubber. Good quality book-style portfolios in the UK are not cheap and can cost anything from £130 to £220. Clearly, if you have a portfolio of this kind, you will not be mailing it out, and will only take it to personal interviews.

An alternative to the book-style portfolio is the portfolio case, which is still more often used by photographers than architects. An important consideration when opting for the portfolio case is its strength and durability. The downside is that it can sometimes be too heavy to be carried around, so try to make it out of lightweight materials. You can be very creative when it comes to the material that you would like to use for your portfolio case – from linen and leather to wood and metal. You can buy it at a store as a ready-made item, or you can have it custom made, and based on your individual needs. Plastic Sandwich (http://www.plasticsandwich.co.uk/) specializes in custom-designed portfolio cases. These cases are made from strong yet lightweight plywood called Israel Gaboon, which is then covered in vinyl. Aluminium portfolio cases are strong, durable and light. Also, they can make a very strong impression, since metal cases are still rarely seen in architectural schools and offices. Aluminum portfolio cases are available in a variety of colours, finishes and styles. The Aluminium Case Company (http://www.aluminiumcases.com/) designs and manufactures a wide range of portfolio cases, which can be custom-foamed to meet individual requirements. Some of their cases, for example, have a slim light panel, which turns the whole portfolio case into a portable light box for a transparency or slide-based portfolio of design work. However, the portfolio container that you buy need not be made for this purpose specifically. You can be creative and buy a ready-made object which can serve as a portfolio container. Erik Heitman, for example, used an old camera as his portfolio container. His work from the University of Kansas was displayed as old-fashioned slides which can be viewed through this camera (see Figures 7.1–7.4).

> **The important thing to consider when buying the right portfolio container is, of course, its price. Bear in mind that some schools will not return your portfolio, or that you might be applying at a number places at the same time, so you might need many portfolios. Before you make any final decisions regarding the right portfolio container, make sure that you know how many portfolios you will need, for what occasions, how you will send them there, and finally whether you will be able to get them back. If you do**

spend a lot of money buying a really beautiful portfolio case, keep in mind that it might not be durable and that you might need to get another one in a couple of years later. Some cases and book style portfolios can decay over time and change colour, so you need to consider how important the issue of durability is for you.

Making a Portfolio Container

Making your own portfolio container can be a longer process, but it can give you more freedom to express your creativity. An inventive and neatly made portfolio case makes an excellent first impression, which is the biggest advantage of making over buying. You can make many types of portfolio containers – cases, binders, folders, etc.

Before you make your final container, make sure to do a mock-up to ensure that your container will actually work and that it will be easy

Figure 7.1
Erik Heitman, Architectural Portfolio, Second Year, B.Arch Programme, University of Kansas, Instructor Christine Huber, Camera Obscura - the portfolio container and its manual

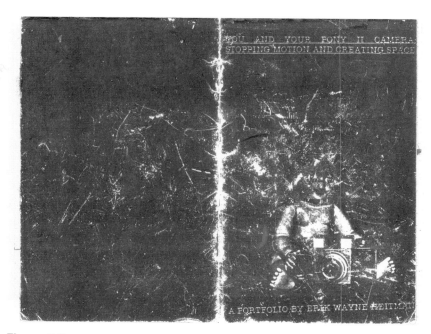

Figure 7.2
Erik Heitman, Architectural Portfolio - User's Guide, cover page

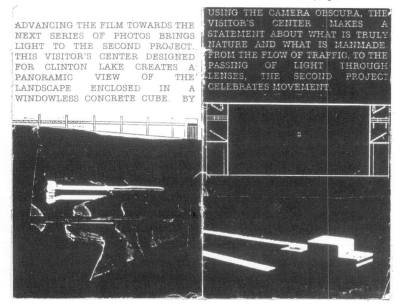

ADVANCING THE FILM TOWARDS THE NEXT SERIES OF PHOTOS BRINGS LIGHT TO THE SECOND PROJECT. THIS VISITOR'S CENTER DESIGNED FOR CLINTON LAKE CREATES A PANORAMIC VIEW OF THE LANDSCAPE ENCLOSED IN A WINDOWLESS CONCRETE CUBE. BY

USING THE CAMERA OBSCURA, THE VISITOR'S CENTER MAKES A STATEMENT ABOUT WHAT IS TRULY NATURE AND WHAT IS MANMADE. FROM THE FLOW OF TRAFFIC, TO THE PASSING OF LIGHT THROUGH LENSES, THE SECOND PROJECT CELEBRATES MOVEMENT.

Figure 7.3
Erik Heitman, Architectural Portfolio - User's Guide

Figure 7.4
Erik Heitman, Architectural Portfolio - portfolio of work

Figure 7.5
Matthew Springett, diploma portfolio container

Figure 7.6
Matthew Springett, diploma portfolio container

Figure 7.7
Andrew Gilles, portfolio container, closed

Figure 7.8
Andrew Gilles, portfolio container, half-opened

Figure 7.9
Andrew Gilles, portfolio container, fully opened

to use. Practice making prototypes, look for interesting examples, not only of different portfolios but also of inventive commercial packaging. An open mind can give you unexpected clues as to how to design an interesting container. And remember – a badly crafted portfolio is professional suicide! Be clean and neat, use the finest materials you can afford, sharp Exacto knives and the finest glue.

Similar to the bought portfolio container, the ease of use in a self-made portfolio is really important. Do not make your portfolio complicated to open or look through – remember that the people looking at your portfolio, even if they may be fascinated by it, will have very little time. Use light materials so one person can handle it easily. Do not

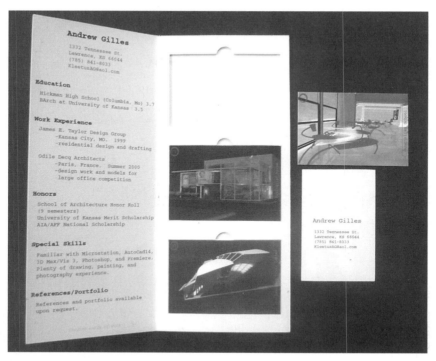

Figure 7.10
Andrew Gilles, résumé and business card holder

make it too big, because that will make it hard to use and mail. Be creative when it comes to the selection of materials and think how the material relates to your work! You can use wood or card, metal, plastic, cloth, etc., and the best choice will be one that makes a link between the work in the portfolio and the portfolio case. You can buy most of these materials at various art stores, but you can also get them at hardware or DIY stores, or even junkyards. We repeat – be inventive, think of some unusual materials, or at least of some unusual combination of materials. A shortage of money can lead you to be particularly inventive here.

You can also play with colour, and paint your portfolio so that it becomes more eye-catching. Your portfolio case might go through a lot of abuse during the review process. With this in mind, try to make it as durable and as abuse-resistant as possible. Use only the best quality materials and paint (yacht quality is usually the most durable), and always check how much pressure it can sustain or how much

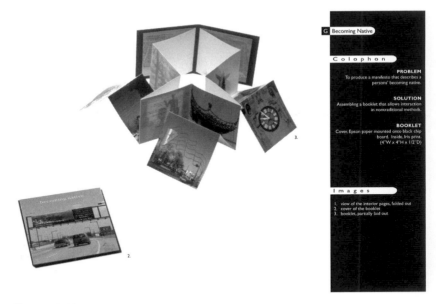

Figure 7.11
Anthony Max D. Marty, portfolio, photo of the project container

Figure 7.12
Anthony Max D. Marty, portfolio, photo of the project container

flipping it can handle so that flipping does not damage it. Andrew Gilles' portfolio container is made as a complex architectural model, so it folds and opens in various directions (see Figures 7.7–7.10). It also containes a custom-made folder for Andrew's business cards, that are again specially designed to match the projects in his portfolio. Anthony Marty's portfolio demonstrates a variety of inventive portfolio containers used to display his academic work (see Figures 7.11 and 7.12).

When it comes to cost, you will need to consider two different types of cost when making your own portfolio. First, you have to do some research about the cost of actual materials and tools. Then, you also have to calculate how much time it will take to make a nicely designed and well-crafted portfolio case – when it comes to application deadlines, time is also money! Finally, when making the case, think also how you are going to mail the portfolio. Investigate standard packages or padded envelopes so that your portfolio fits snugly within. You may need to adjust the size slightly to make a really good fit. Alternately, you can teach yourself how to make a nice mailing package for the portfolio – again seeing time as a form of money before deciding which route you will take.

8 Making the Traditional Portfolio

The layout of your portfolio is as important as its container and its contents. The appropriate use of text, the compositional ideas that orchestrate the relationship between image and text, the use of colour and texture, all contribute to the way your work is received and understood. In this chapter we will introduce you to some basic design issues in making a traditional portfolio, which are also relevant to the following chapter on the digital portfolio.

Graphic Design

The portfolio is your graphic professional résumé. It shows examples of the type and quality of work you have done in the past. It is also an indication of the type of work you can do in the future. Having decided what you wish to include in your portfolio, you will need to think about the sequence and organization of that material. The moment you become involved in the visual organization of images and text, you will be using basic principles of graphic design. One rule of thumb about the sequence of work in a portfolio suggests placing your very best items first and last. Unless you know with total certainty that your audience will look at your portfolio one page at a time, a typical reading pattern will be to glance at the first few samples, then thumb through to the back. The 'best first and last' method ensures that someone can see you in the best possible light in the ten or twenty seconds you may have to make a first impression. It is generally not a good idea to organize your work in chronological order, as that would mean putting your first (and probably weakest) work first.

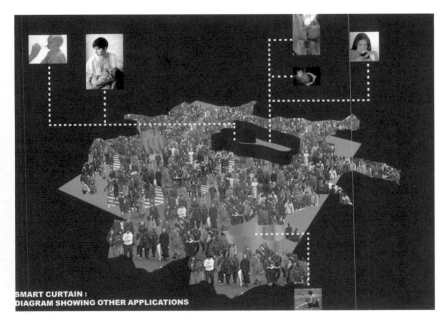

Figure 8.1
Clare Lyster, Smart Curtain, diagram and collage

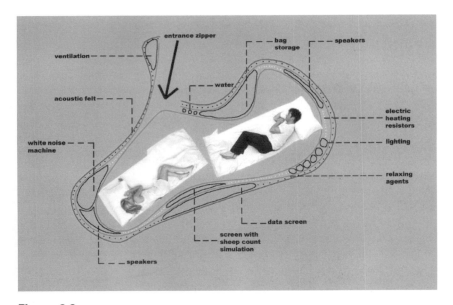

Figure 8.2
Clare Lyster, Smart Curtain, plan diagram and collage

Figure 8.3
Katrin Klingenberg, Daniel Szwaj, Hubertus Hillinger, Pier 42, layered
traditional drawing combining images, lines, and distorted perspective

Integrating Image and Text

Having decided upon the sequence of work, the first and most important graphic design challenge is how to integrate image and text so that
it communicates your ideas as powerfully and clearly as possible.
When you make the first mock-up version of your portfolio, there is a
high possibility that you will end up with isolated rectangles of images
and text. The first rule is to break the traditional separation of image
and text and to blur the boundaries between the two, so that you can
use words to highlight visual ideas, and use visual ideas in the most
effective sequence to construct a narrative in its own right. You can
overlay individual images or image sequences with short paragraphs,
quick title texts or longer bodies of text, depending on whether you are
trying to get a two-second, a ten-second or a forty-five-second idea
across. Think of text as a text, but think of it also as an image that will
enhance your portfolio and clarify your ideas, and think of them both
as having a time-frame within which it can have an affect.

> **However, do NOT put too much text in the portfolio. Remember, your
> audience is unlikely to have a forty-five second chunk of time to study
> your portfolio in detail, unless, of course, you have previously
> completely seduced it into a total immersion in your work.**

Generally, include only the most essential textual explanation for each
project, or part of the project – architects are visual people and will
respond more easily to a plethora of images than to masses of text. You
will notice that some of the portfolio pages included as illustrations in this
book have no text at all – that is perfectly acceptable as long as you introduce each project with enough text for your audience to be able to understand its basic intentions and follow the development of the project
through its visual elements. At a minimum it is helpful to give some
general information, such as the title of the project, its site, the programme, etc. Thereafter, you can rely on the visual strengths of the
design to communicate your ideas. If you wish, you can include quotes
from some of your favourite architectural designers or theorists. This will
suggest some of the sources of your ideas and highlight your ability to
expand your design skills beyond the constraints of a course assignment.

Font Types

Fonts can support or contradict the message in your work. Choosing
the right font type, size and character for different functions in your

portfolio is crucial. First, unless your work is wildly eclectic in its visual elements, it is generally a good idea to use one, or at the most, two fonts in your portfolio. In architecture, text is usually seen as subservient to images, so drawing too much attention to too many font types can be distracting. Second, it is useful having a hierarchy of font sizes for different purposes. Titles and dates of projects in your portfolio should all have one font size. Project descriptions, which should be brief, should have a smaller font size. Drawing or image titles should have a third font size, usually smaller still, but this will depend on your design. If you include quotations in your portfolio, these may have yet another font size or be in italics. Look at competition-winning panels to see how different architects locate and balance block areas of text and use font size to create a hierarchy of information on the page. Third, be consistent as to how you range your text. Will it range from the right, the left, be centred? Will it snake across the drawings? Will it strengthen and fade? Will it rain down across the work? All of these options should be considered carefully in relation to the ideas you are trying to emphasize in the portfolio.

Finally, however, the most important decision you will make about the font will be the font type. Most architects use text in support of images, and do not like to draw attention to the formal qualities of the font itself. For this reason, you will find many architects using fonts that are seen to be relatively visually neutral, like Helvetica or Arial. Other architects like to subtly reinforce the visual message of the work, and choose appropriate fonts to do so. So, if you have a portfolio that is full of the most up-to-date digital imagery, it is unlikely that you will use Book Antiqua or Geometric but might instead want to try AvanteGarde or Gill Sans. If you are trying to get a job in an office that specializes in repair and renovation to historic buildings, and you have a wonderful measured drawing in your portfolio, you might want to use ENGRAVERS GOTHIC or another font that has historical connotations.

Layout and Labelling

The layout of your portfolio should be simple, consistent and inventive. However, it should not be distracting. Your portfolio is certainly an exercise in graphic design, but you shouldn't let the graphics be stronger than your own design work. The layout will also depend on the format used and on the orientation of your boards (portrait or landscape).

Your layout should be organized so that it brings together images and text, using a visual element that is consistent between them. This can be an image, a bit of text or another visual element, which should serve as the main reference on your boards and keeps repeating with some variations to it – a line, a background image, a row of images, a repeated element of text in a specific font, a gestural splash of colour, and so on. Whichever element you decide to use, it should

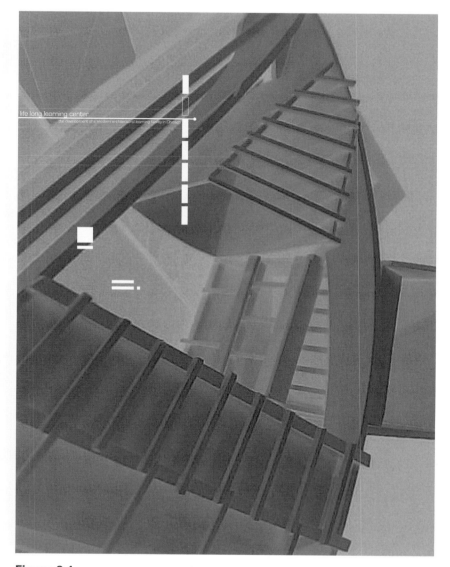

Figure 8.4
Christopher Ciraulo, Life Long Learning Center

relate to the ideas in your portfolio. Figure 8.4 shows an interesting title page layout which, with slight variations, introduces every new project in Christopher Ciraulo's portfolio of work from the University of Illinois at Chicago. Marjan Colletti's unusual use of font and images of toys bring a seductive and provocative quality to the portfolio of work that he produced during his studies at the Bartlett School of Architecture, University College London (see Figure 8.5). Igor Marjanović's portfolio from the University of Illinois at Chicago shows a more geometrically structured organization, which revolves around horizontality and a line that repeats to form a main visual reference element on each board (Figures 8.6 and 8.7).

In all the drawings, plans, sections and details, my friends the softtoys re-appear in the shapes of the 'Bosking'.

Figure 8.5
Marjan Colletti, M.Arch portfolio, The Bartlett School of Architecture, London, UK

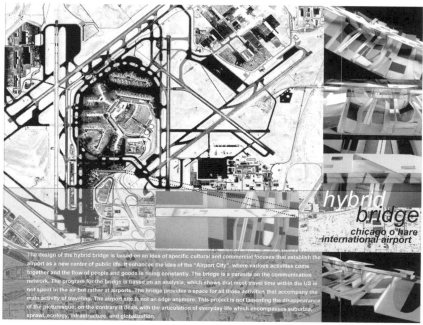

The design of the hybrid bridge is based on an idea of specific cultural and commercial focuses that establish the airport as a new center of public life. It enhances the idea of the "Airport City", where various activities come together and the flow of people and goods is rising constantly. The bridge is a parasite on the communication network. The program for the bridge is based on an analysis, which shows that most travel time within the US is not spent in the air but rather at airports. The bridge provides a space for all those activities that accompany the main activity of traveling. The airport site is not an edge anymore. This project is not lamenting the disappearance of the picturesque; on the contrary it deals with the articulation of everyday life which encompasses suburbia, sprawl, ecology, infrastructure, and globalization.

hybrid bridge
chicago o'hare international airport

Figure 8.6
Igor Marjanović, The Hybrid Bridge, M.Arch thesis project, University of Illinois at Chicago, UIC/SOM Award

Labelling is very important. Without labelling your audience will find it much harder to know what you are trying to emphasize. You should appropriately label all your projects – including the project name, location, drawing type and so on. Be creative with your labels, and think of them as opportunities to make a creative image–text relationship. You want your portfolio to be easy to use and navigate, but you also want to step away from conventional architectural drawings, to create a split second when your audience is both captivated and intrigued, wanting to find out more. You need to use the five-second moment, when you capture your audience's attention, to lead it to the fifteen-second moment, and then to the forty-five-second moment. If your audience is still with you then, you have them with you for the rest of the portfolio. Text, if it really runs in concert with your images, can help you do that. Experiment with text – if you have not had much exposure to graphic design at school then look at all the sources that you find inspiring.

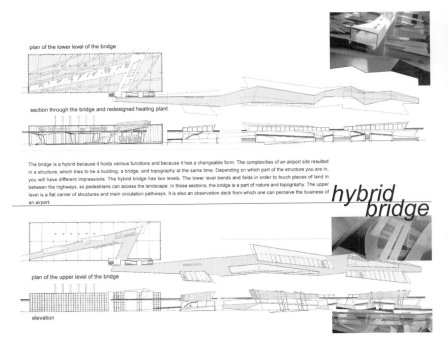

plan of the lower level of the bridge

section through the bridge and redesigned heating plant

The bridge is a hybrid because it hosts various functions and because it has a changeable form. The complexities of an airport site resulted in a structure, which tries to be a building, a bridge, and topography at the same time. Depending on which part of the structure you are in, you will have different impressions. The hybrid bridge has two levels. The lower level bends and folds in order to touch pieces of land in between the highways, so pedestrians can access the landscape. In those sections, the bridge is a part of nature and topography. The upper level is a flat carrier of structures and main circulation pathways. It is also an observation deck from which one can perceive the business of an airport.

hybrid bridge

plan of the upper level of the bridge

elevation

Figure 8.7
Igor Marjanović, The Hybrid Bridge, montage of traditional drawings and model photos

Colour and Textures

Colour can enhance the experience of your portfolio. You can play with colour by printing your portfolio in various tones and hues, but you can also use actual paint and coloured film. For example, even when you print from the computer, you can still use your craft skills to add additional layers of information on your boards. Acrylic and oil colours can easily be applied on many types of printing paper. You can also put a layer of mylar (film) over your boards and start drawing or tracing parts of your portfolio on a new layer. You can also use different textures of paper – matt, glossy, heavyweight, etc. The selection of paper should be closely related to the type of images you will be using on your boards and the kind of effect you would like to produce. The wonderful thing about a portfolio is that it is still, in most cases, a physical object, and most architects work on physical buildings so will appreciate your efforts to express ideas through manipulating surface and grain.

> If you can suggest through your portfolio that you have a real sense for the balance of colour and texture, you will have gone a long way in capturing the attention of an architectural audience.

Assembling the Portfolio

The golden rule of assembling the portfolio is: aim for craft excellence! The way you put your portfolio together speaks not only of your skills, but also of your ability to complete the project with great attention to detail. If you notice that the quality of paper is not good enough, or that it might decay in a short period of time, you should dry mount your boards on thicker paper. Do not spray mount – you cannot predict humidity in the places where your porfolio will be viewed, and humidity makes spray-mounted work bubble and curl in a way that really destroys its quality. Dry mounting (which uses heat to bond one surface to another) is far more expensive than spray mounting, so make sure you only use it when you have to. Dry mounting will also make your portfolio more resistant to both use and abuse. Especially, be careful with photographs and photo quality printing paper, since they tend to be very sensitive. If you spray mount, make sure that photographs are mounted with photo spray mount ONLY – this will help to reduce the dreaded bubbles! Prints from ink jet printers are particularly sensitive to water and spray mounts – dry mount if you can. Finally, when selecting the printing paper for your portfolio, try to use the more durable types, as some brands might decay very quickly and turn yellow even after only a week or two.

The equipment you will need to assemble a well-crafted portfolio will be your standard design studio drafting and model-making equipment, plus your computer, printer and its accessories. You will want to be especially careful with cutting and pasting. Your portfolio should look as clean and neat as possible. When cutting the boards in your portfolio, use only sharp and NEW knives. Keep changing blades – if you have ragged edges in your portfolio you will immediately be seen as a sloppy person, who does not care about detail, and very few schools or offices will accept that. Print on a bigger format than your final portfolio, so that when you are spray mounting and cutting you have enough room for manoeuvring, and trimming your images. Finally, assume that you will make mistakes. Make sure you have enough material to allow you to do everything twice. The best portfolio, like the best project, is made more than once. You will almost never get it right the first time. Allow yourself to fail in private, with nobody around, and then give yourself time to do it again, to a much higher standard. If you can plan for the extra time, make your portfolio for the third time, even better – it will be truly wonderful.

9 The Digital Portfolio

Digital portfolios are becoming more and more common in both the professional and academic spheres. When making a digital portfolio, much of the advice we have given for the traditional portfolio also applies, particularly with respect to the graphic design of the pages, the relationship of images to text, and the use of colour and texture. However, the digital portfolio comes with new aesthetic, technical and organizational possibilities of its own. This chapter will help to introduce you to some of these.

Digital versus 'Traditional' Portfolios

Many schools will give you the option of submitting an electronic portfolio for admission to the graduate programme. Before you decide to go with this option, contact the school's admission office and check in details about what kind of files they expect.

An electronic portfolio offers a large number of possibilities, depending on which software you are using. Most importantly, your portfolio should be easy to read, easy to navigate, and user-friendly. Bear in mind that you are not going to be present while a third party reviews your portfolio and therefore you will not be able to help someone navigate through your work. Assume that some members of your audience will not be as computer-savvy as you. That means your portfolio navigation will have to be incredibly simple. However, at the same time your portfolio still needs to show a level of design and visual excellence that is expected from the traditional portfolio. So, the biggest challenge you are facing is to make things simple and easy to use, but still to make them as beautiful and as original as possible.

Originality is very important when it comes to digital portfolios, since some software applications can give very similar visual results. Similar to the traditional portfolio, try to make your digital portfolio expressive of your personality and interests. Marjan Colletti and Marcos Cruz's portfolio from University College London shows originality through use of unusual fonts and forms (see Figures 9.1 and 9.2). Anthony Halawith's digital portfolio from the University of Illinois at Urbana-Champaign works like a playful and very inviting website (see Figures 9.3 and 9.4). Ryan Knock's CD cover for his digital portfolio of works from the University of Kansas demonstrates interest in buildings, while combining strengths of traditional model making with digital graphics (see Figures 9.5 and 9.6).

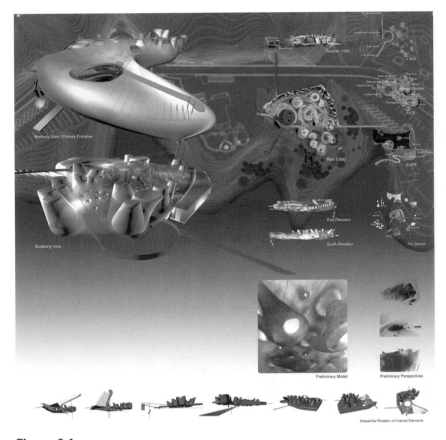

Figure 9.1
Marcosandmarjan, Studio, London, UK, digital portfolio as a montage of 3D renderings and plan diagrams

The Garden of Vessels

Competition proposal for the
New Tomihiro Museum, Japan, 2002.

To visit the New Tomihiro Museum of SHI-GA
is to enter a reinterpreted landscape.
The meandering route presents a process of
discovery, a metaphorical life journey of
Tomihiro himself. Passing through, and between, numerous and varying exhibition
vessels the experience is one of incidences of confluence and activity interspersed with
moments of contemplation and intimacy. Travelling along suspended paths the
sensation of floating, parallel to artworks 'floating' against their neutral landscape,
is communicated. Continuing beyond the physical boundaries of the Museum, specific
paths provide connections to the forest above and the lake below. The possibility of a
real encounter with surrounding nature is raised. An internalised garden, separating
the exhibition spaces from the rest of the Museum, allows for visual awareness of seasonal
change; rain, snow, and blossom falling 'within' the museum.
The external envelope coalesces these elements, transparent and occasionally translucent,
it is interrupted by the liberal intrusion of light cones. Laminated timber provides the
primary structure. The exhibition vessels consist of a dual layered skin, services and
other ancillary requirements existing in the space between. An opaque internal layer
#affords deliberate control of light and humidity, necessary to the environment in
which Tomihiro's work is presented. The existing museum is to be maintained as a
venue for a rotating programme of temporary exhibitions. A new external communal
space is created between it and the new Museum, promoting social activity.
The New Tomihiro Museum of SHI-GA brings together communal interaction and
private introspection. The actual and metaphorical assembly of water, forest, stones and
bridges combine to create a reinterpreted landscape in which to experience the work of
Tomihiro.

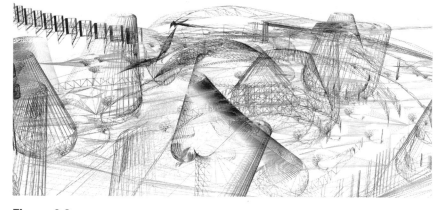

Figure 9.2
Marcosandmarjan, Studio, London, UK, digital portfolio and its narrative

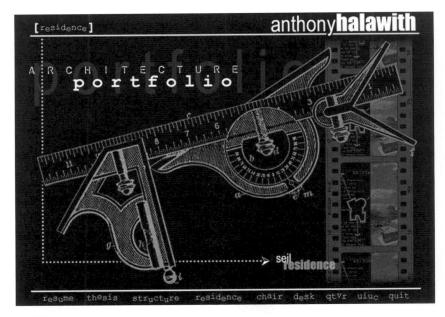

Figure 9.3
Anthony Halawith, digital portfolio #1, main screen

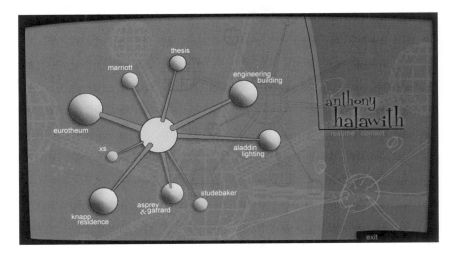

Figure 9.4
Anthony Halawith, digital portfolio #2, main screen

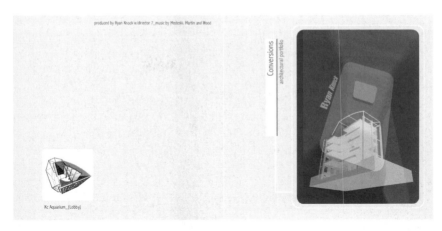

Figure 9.5
Ryan Knock, CD cover #1 for the digital portfolio

Figure 9.6
Ryan Knock, CD cover #2 for the digital portfolio

Digital portfolios can have several formats – they can be on a CD, on a website or simply e-mailed as a document. Whatever format you choose, make sure that your portfolio is a single document. Do not send multiple files as this might cause confusion with the admission committee, creating the risk that someone might simply skip a file. In general, make your files as small as possible, so they can be viewed easily on various platforms. Remember that viewing images on the screen is not the same thing as printing them, which means that the resolution can be quite low, anywhere from 72 dpi to 150 dpi. One of the most important things to bear in mind when it comes to digital portfolios is the difference in platforms (PC, Mac, Unix) and the difference in various browsers. It is good to know how and on what kind of platform your portfolio will be viewed, so you can adjust your portfolio accordingly. If you are not sure, call the school or office and ask! Adobe Photoshop, for example, offers an option to adjust your images to a PC or a Mac palette. So, plan ahead, and eliminate any kind of potential output excuse as to why your digital folio was not working. Similar to the traditional portfolio, you want to be as prepared and as professional as possible.

Sometimes we get too excited about our own digital technology skills and we tend to make the layout and navigation through our portfolio too complicated. This is one of the biggest dangers of a digital portfolio. Do not let the digital technology overcome your design work. Make your portfolio as user friendly as possible. It should be easy to navigate and use. Think of your digital portfolio as if it was a building – it should have the main entrance, corridors, and rooms. From every room you should be able to get back to a corridor or even back to the main entrance. One of the most common mistakes, especially with web-based portfolios, is the omission of a 'home' button, which can take you back to the main menu. The user should be able to navigate back and forth through your portfolio easily and quickly.

Digital portfolio resources:

*   http://www.portfolios.com/ for digital portfolios and creative marketing online,
*   http://www.architosh.com/ for Macintosh based architectural professionals interested in computer technology and digital media
*   http://www.acadia.org/ ACADIA (The Association of the Computer Aided Design in Architecture)
*   http://www.ecaade.org/ eCAADe (Education and research in Computer Aided Architectural Design in Europe)
*   http://www.caadria.org/ CAADRIA (The Association for Computer Aided Architectural Design Research In Asia)
*   http://www.caadfutures.arch.tue.nl/ CAAD Futures

CD Rom

CD Rom stands for 'compact disk read-only memory'. One of the most common formats for a digital portfolio is a CD Rom. The first thing to

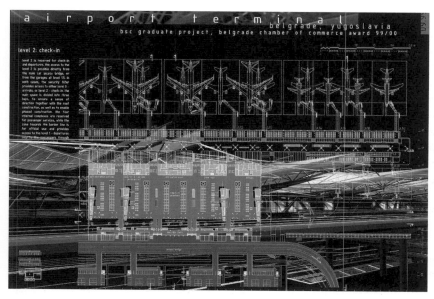

Figure 9.7
Ivan Subanovic, M.Arch thesis project (together with Marcel Ortmans, I Yu, Markus Ruuskanen), Design Research Laboratory, Architectural Association, London, UK

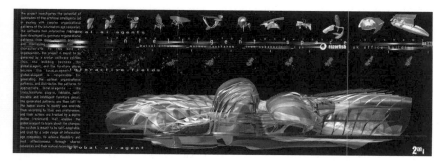

Figure 9.8
Ivan Subanovic, B.Arch thesis project, University of Belgrade, Serbia, Chamber of Commerce Award, 2000

check is to make sure that the CD you are going to use is cross platform compatible, i.e. that it can operate on both PC and Mac platforms. The ISO 9660 CD format should operate on both platforms but do check as new products come on the market all the time. The next important thing is to decide which software you are going to use and how your portfolio will be viewed. Some software is available for free download from the web, so you can include information on your CD saying which software is needed for displaying your portfolio (Adobe Reader, Flash, Shockwave, QuickTime, etc.). Do not, however, assume that your audience will have the time to do this, so

Figure 9.9
Christopher Ciraulo, 3D Softimage renderings

call ahead and check precisely what facilities and software they already have for viewing the CD and fit it to that.

> **This is important advice – always, whatever you do, check the technological capacity of the situation you are trying to enter.**

Generally speaking, there are two types of digital portfolios on a CD – auto play portfolios and the ones through which you can navigate at your own speed by clicking on various menu options. Since the portfolio review always involves some kind of decision-making process that can be lengthy and hard to predict, it is a good idea not to make your portfolio auto play. That way, the admission committee will have the freedom to decide how much time they will spend on various parts of your digital portfolio.

You may also consider doing a DVD portfolio. DVD stands for 'Digital Versatile Disc'. DVDs can have greater capacity to meet a

Figure 9.10
Igor Marjanović, Digital Gallery 1100, Digital Media Institute, University of Illinois at Chicago, montage of Maya animation stills and text

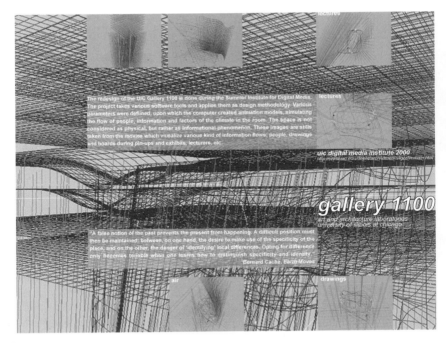

Figure 9.11
Igor Marjanović, Digital Gallery 1100, Digital Media Institute, University of Illinois at Chicago

variety of application needs. Besides being able to download graphic intensive items, DVDs can also run interactive multimedia presentations and/or programs with animations and other interesting video-based components. DVDs are less platform-dependent than a CD Rom and can even be viewed on any TV set without a computer.

Acrobat Reader and PDF files

'PDF' stands for the Adobe® Portable Document Format, which can be created by converting almost any document using Adobe® Acrobat®. This file format is suitable for architectural portfolios and other materials with complex visual designs. Adobe PDF is a universal file format which preserves all the fonts, formatting, graphics, and colour of any source document, regardless of the application and platform used to create it. Adobe PDF files are compact and can be shared, viewed, navigated, and printed exactly as intended by anyone, because

Adobe's® Acrobat® Reader® software can be downloaded free of charge from the web. The format was created to remove machine and platform dependency for its documents, and its goals include design fidelity and typographic control. An Adobe PDF file can be used for printing on PostScript printers or for putting your portfolio on the web. You will find that the Adobe PDF file prints faster than some other types of files and is less likely to cause problems with printing.

Adobe PDF can be used to put your portfolio on the web, where it will have the same consistency of fonts, format, and graphics, regardless of the computer platform. If you are using Adobe PDF to put your portfolio on the web, be aware that it was never designed for interactive online reading – PDF files still lack the speed, simplicity and user control of HTML. However, many word processors, page layout and other graphic design programs can create PDF files easily, so many sites are now using them online. PDF files have a specified page size, for example, and do not re-flow in smaller windows, so people with small screens spend a lot of time scrolling around the window. Another important aspect that affects your decision whether or not to go with Adobe PDF on the web is the use of search engines. When you use most search engines, most of the results you will get come from HTML files and rarely from PDF files. That means that if you are using PDF files, your portfolio might be harder to find through search engines. In order to make your PDF portfolio on the web as search-engine friendly as possible, make sure that each PDF file has correct document properties, especially the title, otherwise it will be hard or even impossible to find it. If possible, break long PDF files into smaller single-subject files, such as project sections, an academic section, a professional practice section, or even chapter sections within the same project.

If at all possible, you should provide both HTML and PDF versions of files, designing the HTML for onscreen use and searching, and PDF for printing only. The good thing is that you can always convert your PDF files to HTML files by using some of the Adobe's® PDF Converters, which are available from their website: www.adobe.com. These products, which convert PDF files to HTML, preserve the structure of the page, graphics, lines, and they even preserve the hyperlinks. However, apart from their Reader, these packages are not free.

Web-based Portfolios

Web presence today is close to an absolute necessity if you wish to generate more than a small circulation for your work, so you should make every effort to build your own site. A personal website with your work and contact details will increase your visibility and potentially connect you to world-wide architectural communities with similar interests or needs. A web page is basically a composite document written in Hypertext Markup Language (HTML) and may contain text, images, hyperlinks (shortcuts to other web pages), drawings, multi-media, etc.

Web-based portfolios are very similar to CD Rom portfolios. One of the things to consider when putting your portfolio on the web is that anyone, anywhere can view it. Decide beforehand whether or not you want your portfolio to be fully accessible or whether you want people to ask for your permission in order to fully review your work. You also have to include information about which version of browser is needed for displaying your work (Netscape and/or Internet Explorer). Check your web page from different platforms (Mac and PC) and different browsers and make sure it works on all of them.

You can also include a copy of your résumé or CV on your web page. You should also have a printable PDF version of your résumé, which can easily be downloaded, printed the way you want it and reviewed.

As architects, we are often too focused on images, and sometimes forget about text. Do not let that happen to you! Always check your spelling. Use simple fonts, either with a serif (Times New Roman) or sans (without) a serif (Arial, Helvetica, Verdana). If you use fonts that are too complicated, the user might not have them installed and that can complicate the review of your work. Always try to eliminate the need for downloading software or fonts in order to review your portfolio – you want to make it as easy to use as possible. Ease of navigation can also be achieved by providing a site search option, or by supplying a site map page, which will list all pages on your website. If you have many pages, and you are concerned that navigation might become a real problem, then you can also provide an index or alphabetical list of your projects, pages, etc. Carefully plan a tour of your website – draw diagrams and envision how someone can navigate through your virtual space. Similar to a traditional portfolio try to start and end with strong projects. Keep the narrative consistent, and use standard graphics and layout.

Image files will be the crucial component of your web-based portfolio. In Chapter 6, we discussed scanning your flat drawings and some of the main image file types. Reduce the size of your images as much as possible, because this will allow for a faster download. You can use a variety of image file formats, but the two most commons types are GIF (Graphics Interchange Format) and JPEG (Joint Photographic Experts Group). The Graphics Interchange Format (GIF) is one of the most popular file formats for Web graphics and for the exchange of graphic files between computers. It is most commonly used for line drawings or blocks of a few distinct colours. In addition, some GIF file formats support transparency, allowing you to make a colour in your image transparent, which can create some very interesting effects in your web portfolio. Please note that while converting an image to GIF, you are also compressing it and changing the original image quality by removing some parts of the original colour information. Be careful – unlike JPEG, GIF does NOT let you control the amount of compression used, so you might end up losing more of the image quality than you actually want to.

The Joint Photographic Experts Group (JPEG) format is another popular format for Web graphics, and is most commonly used for photographs. The JPEG file format stores all colour information in an RGB format (red, green and blue), and then reduces the file size by compressing it, or saving only the colour information that is essential to the image. Keep in mind that the chances of degrading your image when converting it to a JPEG increases proportionally with the amount of compression you use, so try to control the level of compression. As a back-up – always store the original image in case you need it in its original quality and resolution. Unlike some of the GIF file format, JPEGs do not support transparency.

Do not use JPEG for illustrations, cartoons, lettering, or any images that have very sharp edges (i.e. a row of black pixels adjacent to a row of white pixels). Sharp edges in images tend to blur in JPEG format, unless you use only a small amount of compression when converting your image. Such images are better if saved as GIF formats. JPEG is superior to GIF for storing full-colour or grayscale images of 'realistic' scenes. The rule of the thumb is – the more complex the image is, the more likely it is that you will have to use the JPEG file format! You can also use the Portable Network Graphics (PNG) format, which gives full colour, and yet it is very compact. However, this file type is NOT compatible with all browsers.

Desired web technologies include sound, animation, video, etc. They help captivate the audience, while providing a unique experience which cannot be provided by most kinds of traditional portfolios. Sound and video give an additional quality to your web portfolio, but they also increase the size of the file and cause slow downloading. You should keep updating your portfolio and keep testing it. Allow for feedback from the viewers of your work and think how can you use that to improve the quality of your portfolio. And don't forget to include a contact e-mail and your résumé in your website!

10   Afterwards

You have a wonderful portfolio. You have an amazing portfolio case. How then do you send your portfolio so that it arrives without mishap or damage at your destination? The last thing you want is having a damaged portfolio delivered to your destination. You don't want your portfolio to get lost in the mail either. This chapter will help you avoid some of the pitfalls that can confront you once your portfolio is made.

Ways of Sending Your Work

If you are sending a traditional (non-digital portfolio) you must use a reliable carrier, which has a tracking system and a delivery confirmation. Most carriers offer deliveries worldwide, so it is worth shopping around for the best deal. Some destinations might be cheaper or more expensive, depending on the carrier. If you are under pressure to finish and deliver your portfolio by a certain deadline, make sure that the carriers have a next day delivery for that particular postal or zip code. Do not eliminate yourself from the pool of applicants by submitting a late portfolio and/or application. If you are shipping your folios to multiple addresses, make sure you keep track of them and call each institution to verify that it has received them. Some institutions might have limits for the number of pages in your portfolio, so you might want to do some last-minute editing. In order to reduce the cost of shipping your portfolio, you can use light-weight printing paper or a lighter portfolio case, especially if you plan on sending it overseas to multiple addressees. Always call to confirm that your portfolio has arrived in good condition. If it did not, try to negotiate an extension of time, so you can re-send a quality portfolio.

The manner of sending your digital portfolio will depend on the actual format being used. If you are sending a CD, then you might consider designing an interesting and visually exciting CD case (the so-called 'Jewel case'). Make the overall design and layout of the case related to the portfolio design in materials, colour or graphic design. It is also important to pack your CD well and protect it from being damaged in the post. Be aware that CD cases are extremely fragile and can break easily. If you have a website-based portfolio, than there is not much to send via post, except the website address. Nevertheless, you can still be inventive and design a nice postcard or a business card with your website address. Even though your portfolio is a 'paperless one', it always helps to have at least something that can be mailed or 'taken home' as some kind of a reminder of your work. If you are e-mailing your portfolio, always make sure that it reaches its destination and that it could be opened.

> **Make sure that you always have at least one copy of your portfolio with you. If at all possible, do not send originals. Also, give a rough copy of your CV, statement and portfolio, to your referees. Make sure that whoever is writing your letter of recommendations is familiar with the content of your portfolio.**

Finally, do not forget that some institutions will keep your portfolio for their own records; other institutions might send it back to you. Yet other institutions might throw away portfolios after they complete the review process. If you would like to get your portfolio back, make sure that you either provide a self-addressed envelope or simply contact the institutions to verify the procedure for retrieving your portfolio. After spending so much time, effort, energy and money, it would be wise to get your work back for future reference if at all possible.

About the Portfolio Contributors

Mark Chalmers graduated from Kingston University, United Kingdom. He is creative director and founder partner of blueberryfrog, the international advertising agency against traditional ads.

Christopher Ciraulo graduated from the University of Illinois at Chicago School of Architecture with a Bachelor of Arts in Architectural Studies. He is currently a candidate for a Masters of Architecture at the Massachusetts Institute of Technology in Cambridge, USA.

Marjan Colletti graduated from the University of Innsbruck, Austria in 1997 with distinction and received a M.Arch in architectural design with distinction from the Bartlett School of Architecture, UCL London in 1999.

José Gámez received his Ph.D in Architecture and Urban Design from UCLA, his M.Arch from the University of California at Berkeley, and his Bachelor of Environmental Design from Texas A&M University. He is currently an Assistant Professor at the University of North Carolina at Charlotte where he teaches architectural design and cultural theory.

Andrew Gilles graduated from the University of Kansas with a B.Arch honors in 2001. Currently, he is employed at OWP/P Architects in Chicago and is working on several education projects. Awards include AIA/AFF National Scholarship, AIA Medal, and finalist in the City of Chicago's Universal and Affordable Housing Competition.

Anthony Halawith graduated from the University of Illinois at Urbana-Champaign. He is a practicing architect in Chicago.

Erik Heitman earned his Bachelor of Architecture from the University of Kansas with a minor in photography. Currently, he is practising at BNIM Architects of Kansas City, Missouri. His photographic works have been recognized and exhibited by Scholastics and Chicago First Exposure.

Zane Karpova graduated from the University of Illinois at Chicago, Riga Technical University, Latvia and the Norwegian University of Science and Technology. Zane attended UIC as a Fulbright Scholar and in 2002 received the Schiff Foundation Fellowship from the Art Institute of Chicago, as well as the Traveling Fellowship from the SOM Foundation. Currently she is working at Digit-All Studio in Paris and Chicago and co-teaching Digital Media studio.

Katrin Klingenberg graduated from the Leibniz Kolleg in Tuebingen, Technical University in Berlin, Germany and Ball State University, Muncie, Indiana, US, with Diploma and M.Arch degrees. She is a member of the 'Architektenkammer Niedersachsen' in Germany. Currently, she is building the prototype of one of the first 'Passive Houses' in the US in memoriam of Nicolas Smith, who received B.S. and B.Arch degrees from Ball State University, Muncie, Indiana.

Clare Lyster graduated from Yale School of Architecture with an M.Arch Masters degree and from the University College Dublin with a B.Arch degree. She is currently an Adjunct Assistant Professor at the University of Illinois at Chicago, where she was the Alvin Boyarsky Research and Teaching Fellow. She is the recipient of a research bursary from the Arts Council in Ireland.

marcosandmarjan is a London-based studio, founded by Marcos Cruz and Marjan Colletti in 2000. The studio develops experimental architecture and participates in several international competitions and architectural exhibitions, including Bartfest 2002 London, Biennale di Porto Ercole and Galeria Maus Habitos Porto.

Anthony Max D. Marty practices graphic design at Grady Campbell of Chicago, Illinois. He received his B.Arch from the Illinois Institute of Technology, where he was the recipient of the Samuel Horowitz Award. His photographs and furniture designs have been exhibited in a number of Chicago galleries.

Rahman Polk obtained his B.Arch from the University of Illinois at Chicago. He is currently teaching architectural design at the UIC while working at Hammond Beeby Rupert Ainge, Inc. He has an Honorable Mention (with Byron Terrell) in the TKTS2K Design Competition sponsored by the Van Alen Institute.

Research Experiment Design (RED) was formed in London in the early 2001 by a group of graduates from the Architectural Association DRL, are Elie Abs, Thomas Heidingsfelder, Antonio Ramirez and

Djordje Stojanović. RED is currently working in Europe and the Middle East.

Matthew Springett graduated from the Bartlett School of Architecture with the Banister Fletcher medal and the Royal Institute of British Architects Silver Medal. He is design tutor at the Bartlett School of Architecture with Kirsteen Mackay. In 2000 Springett Mackay Architecture (SMA) was formed, and was recently awarded the Best First-time Exhibitor prize at the Royal Academy of Arts.

Ivan Subanovic (BSc, MArch) graduated from the University of Belgrade and graduated with highest honours from the Architectural Association in London. He is currently working for the London based firm Wilkinson Eyre Architects.

Index

Architectural Press

An imprint of Elsevier Science
www.architecturalpress.com

Visit www.architecturalpress.com

Our regularly updated website includes:

- News on our latest books
- Special offers, discounts and freebies
- Free downloadable sample chapters from our newest titles
- Links to companion websites giving you extra information on our books
- Author biographies and information
- Links to useful websites and extensive directories of relevant organisations and publications
- A search engine and a secure online ordering system for the entire catalogue of **Architectural Press** books

You can also get **free membership** of our **eNews** service by visiting our website to register. Once you are a member, you will receive a monthly email bulletin which gives you:

- Exclusive author articles
- The chance to enter prize draws for free books
- Access to offers and discounts exclusive to **eNews** members
- News of our latest books sent direct to your desktop

If you would like any other information about **www.architecturalpress.com** or our **eNews** service please contact:

Rachel Lace, Product Manager
Email: r.lace@elsevier.com
Tel: +44 (0) 1865 314594
Fax: +44 (0)1865 314572
Address: Architectural Press, Linacre House, Jordan Hill, Oxford, OX2 8DP, UK